for Sister Maryanna
my treasured friend — ♡ **W9-ASA-235**

Lovingly. Eve

May 11 - 1986

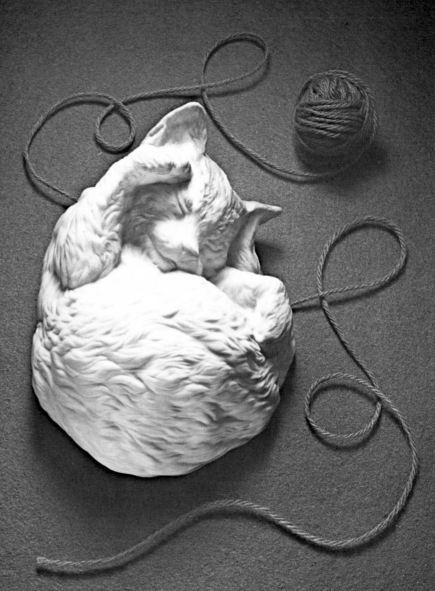

A Kitten

He's nothing much but fur
And two round eyes of blue,
He has a giant purr
And a midget mew.

He darts and pats the air,
He starts and pricks his ear,
When there is nothing there
For him to see and hear.

He runs around in rings,
But why we cannot tell;
With sideways leaps he springs
At things invisible—

Then half-way through a leap
His startled eyeballs close,
And he drops off to sleep
With one paw on his nose.

ELEANOR FARJEON

Poems for Children
and Other People

Edited by George Hornby

ILLUSTRATED WITH CYBIS PORCELAIN SCULPTURES

CROWN PUBLISHERS, INC. : NEW YORK

Library of Congress Cataloging in Publication Data
Main entry under title:

Poems for children and other people.
    Includes indexes.
    SUMMARY: An anthology of poetry by such poets as Hardy,
Field, Lear, Frost, Dickinson, Southey, Whittier, Blake, Carroll,
and many more.
    1. English poetry. 2. American poetry. [1. Poetry—Collec-
tions] 1. Hornby, George Arthur, 1911—   II. Cybis, Inc.
PR1175.P623   821′.008   75-35971
ISBN 0-517-52588-7

Fourth Printing, December, 1976

A George Hornby Book

COPYRIGHT ACKNOWLEDGMENTS

"The Rivals" by James Stephens. From *Collected Poems*, copyright 1915 by Macmillan Publishing Co., Inc., renewed 1943 by James Stephens. Reprinted by permission of Macmillan Publishing Co., Inc. and The Macmillan Company of Canada Limited.

"Little Things" by James Stephens. From *Collected Poems*, copyright 1926 by Macmillan Publishing Co., Inc., renewed 1954 by Cynthia Stephens. Reprinted by permission of Macmillan Publishing Co., Inc. and The Macmillan Company of Canada Limited.

"Dance of Burros" by Dilys Laing. From *Poems from a Cage*, copyright 1952 by Alexander Laing. Reprinted by permission of Macmillan Publishing Co., Inc.

"To a Squirrel at Kyle-Na-No" by William Butler Yeats. From *The Collected Poems of W. B. Yeats*, copyright 1919 by Macmillan Publishing Co., Inc., renewed 1947 by Bertha Georgie Yeats. Reprinted by permission of Macmillan Publishing Co., Inc., M. B. Yeats, Miss Ann Yeats, Macmillan Company of London and Basingstoke and A. P. Watt & Son.

"Emily Dickinson" by Melville Cane. From *So That It Flower*, copyright, 1938, 1966, by Melville Cane. Reprinted by permission of Harcourt Brace Jovanovich, Inc.

"Splinter" by Carl Sandburg. From *Good Morning, America*, copyright, 1928, 1956, by Carl Sandburg. Reprinted by permission of Harcourt Brace Jovanovich, Inc.

"Buffalo Dusk" by Carl Sandburg. From *Smoke and Steel* by Carl Sandburg, copyright, 1920, by Harcourt Brace Jovanovich, Inc.; copyright, 1948, by Carl Sandburg. Reprinted by permission of the publishers.

"Lilacs" by Amy Lowell. From *The Complete Poetical Works of Amy Lowell*. Copyright 1955, by Houghton Mifflin Company. Reprinted by permission of the publishers.

"The Last Word of a Bluebird" by Robert Frost. From *The Poetry of Robert Frost* edited by Edward Connery Lathem. Copyright 1916, © 1969 by Holt, Rinehart and Winston, Inc. Copyright 1944 by Robert Frost. Reprinted by permission of Holt, Rinehart and Winston, Publishers.

"A Kitten" by Eleanor Farjeon. Copyright 1933, © renewed 1961 by Eleanor Farjeon. From *Poems for Children* by Eleanor Farjeon. Copyright 1951 by Eleanor Farjeon. Reprinted by permission of J. B. Lippincott Company.

"The Flower-Fed Buffaloes" by Vachel Lindsay. Copyright by Elizabeth C. Lindsay from the book *Going to the Stars*. Reprinted by permission of the estate of Vachel Lindsay.

"An Explanation of the Grasshopper" by Vachel Lindsay. From *Collected Poems*, copyright 1914 by Macmillan Publishing Co., Inc., renewed 1942 by Elizabeth C. Lindsay. Reprinted by permission of Macmillan Publishing Co., Inc.

"The Little Turtle" by Vachel Lindsay. From *Collected Poems*, copyright 1920 by Macmillan Publishing Co., Inc., renewed 1948 by Elizabeth C. Lindsay. Reprinted by permission of Macmillan Publishing Co., Inc.

"Mirror for Myself" and "Lily-Bell" by Roger Wescott. Reprinted by permission of the author. All rights reserved.

"Chamber Music" by James Joyce. From *Collected Poems*, 1918, 1927. The Viking Press, Inc. Reprinted by permission of the publishers.

"Serious Omission" by John Farrar. From *Songs for Parents*, copyright 1921 by Yale University Press. Reprinted by permission of the publishers.

To Emily Dickinson

Inclosed within a hedge
Of privet, doubts and nays,
A burning spinster paced
Her clipped New England days.

While pretty singers droned
A local, nasal hymn,
She raised a timeless voice;
It reached the spatial rim.

She never saw a moor,
She never saw the sea,
Yet from a hilltop in her heart
She scanned Infinity.

MELVILLE CANE

Table of Contents

List of Illustrations

An Introductory Note

Go, little book, and wish to all
Flowers in the garden, meat in the hall,
A bit of wine, a spice of wit,
A house with lawns enclosing it,
A living river by the door,
A nightingale in the sycamore!

R.L.S.

SOME of us never grow old and some of us, unfortunately, were never young. Poets have always known this. Hence this selection and its title. There is here no rigid grading and not all are great or famous poems. But all of them will sing to some readers and, perhaps, whisper to the "other people." The porcelains of Cybis are beautiful complements to the poems. Some tell a story. Some capture a moment in time. All evoke a sense of poetry. Some are priceless pieces for the captains and kings of the world and there are some little pieces of equal joy but more modest in aim.

Without the sculptures that decorate it this little book would be merely another minor anthology. With them we have a rare communion of arts. A joining that began the day I visited the Cybis studios and found artists making poetry out of clay.

The sensitive artistry of Cybis Porcelains reflects the techniques and devotions of the early master craftsmen. This is not surprising when one realizes that the firm's originator, Boleslaw Cybis, an internationally known sculptor and painter, spent some of his formative years in the old Saxony country-side near Meissen. Dedicated to creating memorable sculptures for the connoisseur and collector, Cybis remains a small and disciplined group of American artists who understand and practice the old world methods. In the Cybis Studio each Porcelain is individually crafted and no two are ever exactly alike. Each sculpture bearing the Cybis imprimatur carries within it something of the pleasure and devotion of the artists who helped to create it.

I wish to give very special credit to my wife, Veronica, not just for the encouragement she has always given me but for specific help in the research, assembling, and indexing of this little volume. To my assistant, Huguette Franco, credit for help beyond the call of duty in the execution of my rough design and layout. My associates at Crown know I appreciate their help and encouragement. To the artists of Cybis go my thanks and admiration.

G.H.

Growing Things

Flower in the crannied wall,
I pluck you out of the crannies,
I hold you here, root and all, in my hand,
Little flower—but *if* I could understand
What you are, root and all, and all in all,
I should know what God and man is.

ALFRED, LORD TENNYSON

Stars and Flowers

If stars dropped out of heaven,
   And if flowers took their place,
The sky would still look very fair,
   And fair earth's face.

Winged angels might fly down to us
   To pluck the stars,
But we could only long for flowers
   Beyond the cloudy bars.

CHRISTINA ROSSETTI

The City Child

Dainty little maiden, whither would you
    wander?
Whither from this pretty home, the home where
    mother dwells?
"Far and far away," said the dainty little maiden,
"All among the gardens, auriculas, anemones,
Roses and lilies and Canterbury bells."

Dainty little maiden, whither would you
    wander?
Whither from this pretty house, this city-house
    of ours?
"Far and far away," said the dainty little maiden,
Whither from this pretty house, this city-house
    of ours??
"Far and far away," said the dainty little maiden,
"All among the meadows, the clover and the
    clematis,
Daisies and kingcups and honeysuckle-flowers."

ALFRED, LORD TENNYSON

Time to Rise

A birdie with a yellow bill
Hopped upon the window sill,
Cocked his shining eye and said:
"Ain't you 'shamed, you sleepy-head!"

ROBERT LOUIS STEVENSON

Wrens and robins in the hedge,
    Wrens and robin here and there;
Building, perching, pecking, fluttering,
    Everywhere!

CHRISTINA ROSSETTI

Spring Flower

Daffy-down-dilly has come up to town
In yellow petticoat and a green gown.

❧

Pansy

Of all the bonny buds that blow
  In bright or cloudy weather,
Of all the flowers that come and go
  The whole twelve months together,
This little purple pansy brings
Thoughts of the sweetest, saddest things.

MARY E. BRADLEY

❧

Flower Piece

Heart's ease or pansy, pleasure or thought,
Which would the picture give us of these?
Surely the heart that conceived it sought
  Heart's ease.

ALGERNON CHARLES SWINBURNE

❧

To the Small Celandine

Pansies, lilies, kingcups, daisies,
Let them live upon their praises;
  Long as there's a sun that sets,
    Primrose will have their glory;
  Long as there are violets,
    They will have a place in story:
There's a flower that shall be mine,
'Tis the little Celandine.

Ere a leaf is on a bush,
In the time before the thrush
  Has a thought about her nest,
    Thou wilt come with half a call,
  Spreading out thy glossy breast
    Like a careless Prodigal;
Telling tales about the sun,
When we've little warmth, or none.

WILLIAM WORDSWORTH

Daisies

Where innocent bright-eyed daisies are,
  With blades of grass between,
Each daisy stands up like a star,
  Out of a sky of green.

CHRISTINA ROSSETTI

The Elf
and the Dormouse

Under a toadstool
  Crept a wee Elf,
Out of the rain
  To shelter himself.

Under the toadstool,
  Sound asleep,
Sat a big Dormouse
  All in a heap.

Trembled the wee Elf,
  Frightened, and yet
Fearing to fly away
  Lest he get wet.

To the next shelter—
  Maybe a mile!
Sudden the wee Elf
  Smiled a wee smile,

Tugged till the toadstool
  Toppled in two.
Holding it over him
  Gaily he flew.

Soon he was safe home
  Dry as could be.
Soon woke the Dormouse—
  "Good gracious me!

Where is my toadstool?"
  Loud he lamented.
—And that's how umbrellas
  First were invented.

OLIVER HERFORD

A Tree

In Spring I look gay,
  Decked in comely array,
In summer more clothing I wear;
  When colder it grows
  I fling off my clothes,
And in winter quite naked appear.

To a Butterfly

I've watched you now a full half-hour,
Self-poised upon that yellow flower;
And, little Butterfly! indeed
I know not if you sleep or feed.
How motionless! not frozen seas
More motionless! and then
What joy awaits you, when the breeze
Has found you out among the trees,
And calls you forth again!

This plot of orchard-ground is ours;
My trees they are, my Sister's flowers;
Here rest your wings when they are weary;
Here lodge as in a sanctuary!
Come often to us, fear no wrong;
Sit near us on the bough!
We'll talk of sunshine and of song,
And summer days, when we are young;
Sweet childish days, that were as long
As twenty days are now.

WILLIAM WORDSWORTH

To Daffodils

Fair daffodils, we weep to see
　　You haste away so soon;
As yet the early rising sun
　　Has not attained his noon:
　　　　Stay, stay
　　Until the hastening day
　　　　Has run
　　But to the evensong;
And having prayed together, we
　　Will go with you along!

We have short time to stay, as you,
　　We have as short a spring,
As quick a growth to meet decay,
　　As you or anything.
　　　　We die
　　As your hours do; and dry
　　　　Away,
　　Like to the summer's rain,
Or as the pearls of morning dew,
　　Ne'er to be found again.

ROBERT HERRICK

Buttercups

Buttercups, buttercups
　　Stretching for miles
Through the green meadow-land,
　　Over the stiles.

Buttercups, buttercups,
　　Standing so high
In all the summer grass,
　　Under the sky.

DOLLY RADFORD

Mignonette

A pitcher of mignonette
　　In a tenement's highest casement,—
Queer sort of a flower-pot—yet
That pitcher of mignonette
Is a garden in heaven set
　　To the little sick child in the basement—
The pitcher of mignonette,
　　In the tenement's highest casement.

H. C. BUNNER

From a Calendar

First came the primrose.
On the bank high,
Like a maiden looking forth
From the window of a tower
When the battle rolls below,
So looked she,
And saw the storms go by.

Then came the wind-flower
In the valley left behind,
As a wounded maiden pale
With purple streaks of woe
When the battle has rolled by
Wanders to and fro,
So tottered she,
Dishevelled in the wind.

SYDNEY DOBELL

Loveliest of Trees

Loveliest of trees, the cherry now
Is hung with bloom along the bough,
And stands about the woodland ride
Wearing white for Eastertide.

Now, of my threescore years and ten,
Twenty will not come again,
And take from seventy springs a score,
It only leaves me fifty more.

And since to look at things in bloom
Fifty springs are little room,
About the woodlands I will go
To see the cherry hung with snow.

A. E. HOUSMAN

∽∽∽

To a Little Girl

Her eyes are like forget-me-nots,
    So loving, kind and true;
Her lips are like a pink sea-shell
    Just as the sun shines through;

Her hair is like the waving grain
    In summer's golden light;
And, best of all, her little soul
    Is, like a lily, white.

GUSTAV KOBBÉ

∽∽∽

A Lily of a Day

It is not growing like a tree
    In bulk, doth make man better be;
Or standing long an oak, three hundred year,
To fall a log at last, dry, bald, and sear:
    A lily of a day
    Is fairer far in May,
Although it fall and die that night,—
It was the plant and flower of Light.
In small proportions we just beauties see,
And in short measures life may perfect be.

BEN JONSON

Lily-Bell

Ring, ring the lily-bell!
Now it's dusk, and all is well:
Come and join the fairy-dance
    In the moony dell.

ROGER WESCOTT

17

The Crocus

The golden crocus reaches up
To catch a sunbeam in her cup.
WALTER CRANE

The Little Plant

In the heart of a seed
  Buried deep, so deep,
A dear little plant
  Lay fast asleep.

"Wake!" said the sunshine
  "And creep to the light,"
"Wake!" said the voice
  Of the raindrops bright.

The little plant heard,
  And it rose to see
What the wonderful
  Outside world might be.

KATE LOUISE BROWN

A Garden

A sensitive plant in a garden grew,
And the young winds fed it with silver dew,
And it open'd its fan-like leaves to the light,
And closed them beneath the kisses of night.
And the Spring arose on the garden fair,
And the Spirit of Love fell everywhere;
And each flower and herb on Earth's dark breast
Rose from the dreams of its wintry nest.
The snowdrop, and then the violet,
Arose from the ground with warm rain wet,
And their breath was mix'd with fresh odour, sent
From the turf, like the voice and the instrument.
Then the pied wind-flowers and the tulip tall,
And narcissi, the fairest among them all,
Who gaze on their eyes in the stream's recess,
Till they die of their own dear loveliness.

PERCY BYSSHE SHELLEY

To the Fringed Gentian

Thou blossom bright with autumn dew,
And colored with the heaven's own blue,
That openest when the quiet light
Succeeds the keen and frosty night,

Thou comest not when violets lean
O'er wandering brooks and springs unseen,
Or columbines, in purple dressed,
Nod o'er the ground-bird's hidden nest.

Thou waitest late and com'st alone,
When woods are bare and birds are flown,
And frosts and shortening days portend
The aged year is near his end.

Then doth thy sweet and quiet eye
Look through its fringes to the sky,
Blue—blue—as if that sky let fall
A flower from its cerulean wall.

I would that thus, when I shall see
The hour of death draw near to me,
Hope, blossoming within my heart,
May look to heaven as I depart.

WILLIAM CULLEN BRYANT

The Violet and the Rose

The violet in the wood, that's sweet to-day,
    Is longer sweet than roses of red June;
Set me sweet violets along my way,
    And bid the red rose flower, but not too soon.
Ah violet, ah rose, why not the two?
Why bloom not all fair flowers the whole year
    through?
    Why not the two, young violet, ripe rose?
    Why dies one sweetness when another blows?

AUGUSTA WEBSTER

To a Wind-Flower

Teach me the secret of thy loveliness,
    That, being made wise, I may aspire to be
As beautiful in thought, and so express
    Immortal truths to earth's mortality.

MADISON CAWEIN

19

April Rain

It is not raining rain for me,
   It's raining daffodils;
In every dimpled drop I see
   Wild flowers on the hills.

The clouds of gray engulf the day
   And overwhelm the town;
It is not raining rain to me,
   It's raining roses down.

It is not raining rain to me,
   But fields of clover bloom,
Where any buccaneering bee
   Can find a bed and room.

A health unto the happy,
   A fig for him who frets!
It is not raining rain to me,
   It's raining violets.

ROBERT LOVEMAN

The Violet

Down in a green and shady bed,
   A modest violet grew,
Its stalk was bent, it hung its head,
   As if to hide from view.

And yet it was a lovely flower,
   Its color bright and fair;
It might have graced a rosy bower,
   Instead of hiding there.

Yet there it was content to bloom,
   In modest tints arrayed;
And there diffused its sweet perfume,
   Within the silent shade.

Then let me to the valley go,
   This pretty flower to see;
That I may also learn to grow
   In sweet humility.

JANE TAYLOR

Birds of the Air

Be like the bird, who
Halting in his flight
On limb too slight
Feels it give way beneath him,
Yet sings
Knowing he hath wings.

VICTOR HUGO

My Doves

My little doves have left a nest
   Upon an Indian tree,
Whose leaves fantastic take their rest
   Or motion from the sea;
For, ever there the sea-winds go
With sunlit paces to and fro.

The tropic flowers looked up to it,
   The tropic stars looked down,
And there my little doves did sit
   With feathers softly brown,
And glittering eyes that showed their right
To general Nature's deep delight.

My little doves were ta'en away
   From that glad nest of theirs,
Across an ocean rolling grey,
   And tempest-clouded airs.
My little doves who lately knew
The sky and wave by warmth and blue.

And now, within the city prison
   In mist and chillness pent,
With sudden upward look their listen
   For sounds of past content,
For lapse of water, smell of breeze,
Or nut-fruit falling from the trees.

ELIZABETH BARRETT BROWNING

Bob White

There's a plump little chap in a speckled coat,
And he sings on the zigzag rails remote,
Where he whistles at breezy, bracing, morn,
When the buckwheat is ripe, and stacked
    is the corn,
  "Bob White! Bob White! Bob White!"
Is he hailing some comrade as blithe as he?
Now I wonder where Robert White can be!

O'er the billows of gold and amber grain
There is no one in sight—but, hark again:
Ah! I see why he calls; in the stubble there
Hide his plump little wife and babies fair!
So contented is he, and so proud of the same,
That he wants all the world to know his name:
  "Bob White! Bob White! Bob White!"

GEORGE COOPER

I Heard a Bird Sing

I heard a bird sing
  In the dark of December
A magical thing
  And sweet to remember.

"We are nearer to Spring
  Than we were in September,"
I heard a bird sing
  In the dark of December.

OLIVER HERFORD

The Rivals

I heard a bird at dawn
Singing sweetly on a tree,
That the dew was on the lawn,
And the wind was on the lea;
But I didn't listen to him,
For he didn't sing to me.

JAMES STEPHENS

The Swallow

Fly away, fly away over the sea,
  Sun-loving swallow, for summer is done;
Come again, come again, come back to me,
  Bringing the summer and bringing the sun.

CHRISTINA ROSSETTI

The Swallow's Nest

Day after day her nest she moulded,
  Building with magic, love and mud,
A gray cup made by a thousand journeys,
  And the tiny beak was trowel and hod.

EDWIN ARNOLD

The Building of the Nest

They'll come again to the apple tree—
  Robin and all the rest—
When the orchard branches are fair to see,
  In the snow of the blossoms dressed;
And the prettiest thing in the world will be
  The building of the nest.

Weaving it well, so round and trim,
  Hollowing it with care,—
Nothing too far away for him,
  Nothing for her too fair,—
Hanging it safe on the topmost limb,
  Their castle in the air.

Ah! mother bird, you'll have weary days
  When the eggs are under your breast,
And shadow may darken the dancing rays
  When the wee ones leave the nest;
But they'll find their wings in a glad amaze,
  And God will see to the rest.

So come to the trees with all your train
  When the apple blossoms blow;
Through the April shimmer of sun and rain,
  Go flying to and fro;
And sing to our hearts as we watch again
  Your fairy building grow.

MARGARET SANGSTER

Lilacs

Lilacs,
False blue,
White,
Purple,
Color of lilac,
Your great puffs of flowers
Are everywhere in this my New England.
Among your heart-shaped leaves
Orange orioles hop like music-box birds and sing
Their little weak soft songs;
In the crooks of your branches
The bright eyes of song sparrows sitting on
    spotted eggs
Peer restlessly through the light and shadow
Of all Springs.

AMY LOWELL

The Maryland Yellow-throat

When May bedecks the naked trees
With tassels and embroideries,
And many blue-eyed violets beam
Along the edges of the stream,
I hear a voice that seems to say,
Now near at hand, now far away,
    "Witchery—witchery—witchery."

An incantation so serene,
So innocent, befits the scene:
There's magic in that small bird's note—
See, there he flits—the Yellow-throat;
A living sunbeam, tipped with wings,
A spark of light that shines and sings
    "Witchery—witchery—witchery."

HENRY VAN DYKE

Bird Song

The robin sings of willow-buds,
  Of snowflakes on the green;
The bluebird sings of Mayflowers,
  The crackling leaves between;
The veery has a thousand tales
  To tell to girl and boy;
But the oriole, the oriole,
  Sings, "Joy! joy! joy!"

The pewee calls his little mate,
  Sweet Phœbe, gone astray,
The warbler sings, "What fun, what fun,
  To tilt upon the spray!"
The cuckoo has no song, but clucks,
  Like any wooden toy;
But the oriole, the oriole,
  Sings, "Joy! joy! joy!"

The grosbeak sings the rose's birth,
  And paints her on his breast;
The sparrow sings of speckled eggs,
  Soft brooded in the nest.
The wood-thrush sings of peace, "Sweet peace,
  Sweet peace," without alloy;
But the oriole, the oriole,
  Sings "Joy! joy! joy!"

LAURA E. RICHARDS

Yellow Flutterings

Sometimes goldfinches one by one will drop
From low hung branches; little space they stop;
But sip and twitter, and their feathers sleek;
Then off at once, as in a wanton freak:
Or perhaps, to show their black, and golden wings,
Pausing upon their yellow flutterings.

JOHN KEATS

The Last Word of a Bluebird

As I went out a Crow
In a low voice said 'Oh,
I was looking for you.
How do you do?
I just came to tell you
To tell Lesley (will you?)
That her little Bluebird
Wanted me to bring word
That the north wind last night
That made the stars bright
And made ice on the trough
Almost made him cough
His tail feathers off.
He just had to fly!
But he sent her Good by,
And said to be good,
And wear her red hood,
And look for skunk tracks
In the snow with an ax—
And do everything!
And perhaps in the spring
He would come back and sing.'

ROBERT FROST

The Wood-Dove's Note

Meadows with yellow cowslips all aglow,
   Glory of sunshine on the uplands bare,
And faint and far, with sweet elusive flow,
   The Wood-dove's plaintive call.
       "O where! where! where!"

Straight with old Omar in the almond grove
   From whitening boughs I breathe the odors rare
And hear the princess mourning for her love
   With sad unwearied plaint,
       "O where! where! where!"

New Madrigals in each soft pulsing throat—
   New life upleaping to the brooding air—
Still the heart answers to that questing note,
   "Soul of the vanished years,
       O where! where! where!"

EMILY HUNTINGTON MILLER

"What does Little Birdie Say?"

What does little birdie say
In her nest at peep of day?
Let me fly, says little birdie,
Mother, let me fly away.
Birdie, rest a little longer,
Till the little wings are stronger.
So she rests a little longer,
Then she flies away.

What does little baby say,
In her bed at peep of day?
Baby says, like little birdie,
Let me rise and fly away.
Baby, sleep a little longer,
Till the little limbs are stronger,
If she sleeps a little longer,
Baby too shall fly away.

ALFRED, LORD TENNYSON

The Humming Bird

The sunlight speaks, and its voice is a bird:
It glimmers half-guessed, half-seen, half-heard,
Above the flowerbed, over the lawn—
A flashing dip, and it is gone,
And all it lends to the eye is this—
A sunbeam giving the air a kiss.

HARRY KEMP

The Sandpiper

Across the narrow beach we flit,
    One little sandpiper and I;
And fast I gather, bit by bit,
    The scattered driftwood bleached and dry.
The wild waves reach their hands for it,
    The wild wind raves, the tide runs high,
As up and down the beach we flit,
    One little sandpiper and I.

Above our heads the sullen clouds
    Scud black and swift across the sky;
Like silent ghosts in misty shrouds
    Stand out the white light-houses high.
Almost as far as eye can reach
    I see the close-reefed vessels fly,
As fast we flit along the beach,
    One little sandpiper and I.

I watch him as he skims along
    Uttering his sweet and mournful cry;
He starts not at my fitful song,
    Or flash of fluttering drapery.
He has no thought of any wrong;
    He scans me with a fearless eye.
Stanch friends are we, well tried and strong,
    The little sandpiper and I.

Comrade, where wilt thou be tonight
    When the loosed storm breaks furiously?
My driftwood fire will burn so bright!
    To what warm shelter canst thou fly?
I do not fear for thee, though wroth
    The tempest rushes through the sky:
For are we not God's children both,
    Thou, little sandpiper, and I?

CELIA THAXTER

Herons

A breeze blows o'er the lake;
Against the heron's slender legs
    The little ripples break.

If they had no voices, lo!
White herons would be
    But a line of snow.

JAPANESE HOKKU

29

To a Waterfowl

Whither, midst falling dew,
While glow the heavens with the last steps of day,
Far, through their rosy depths, dost thou pursue
    Thy solitary way?

    Vainly the fowler's eyes
Might mark thy distant flight to do thee wrong,
As, darkly painted on the crimson sky,
    Thy figure floats along.

    Seek'st thou the plashy brink
Of weedy lake, or marge of river wide,
Or where the rocking billows rise and sink
    One the chafed ocean-side?

    There is a Power whose care
Teaches thy way along that pathless coast,—
The desert and illimitable air,—
    Lone wandering but not lost.

    All day thy wings have fanned
At that far height, the cold, thin atmosphere,
Yet stoop not, weary, to the welcome land,
    Though the dark night is near.

    And soon that toil shall end;
Soon shalt thou find a summer home, and rest,
And scream among thy fellows; reeds shall bend.
    Soon, o'er thy sheltered nest.

    Thou'rt gone, the abyss of heaven
Hath swallowed up thy form; yet, on my heart
Deeply hath sunk the lesson thou hast given,
    And shall not soon depart.

    He who, from zone to zone,
Guides through the boundless sky thy certain flight,
In the long way that I must tread alone,
    Will lead my steps aright.

WILLIAM CULLEN BRYANT

The Chickadee

Piped a tiny voice hard by,
Gay and polite, a cheerful cry,
"Chic-chicadee-dee!" Saucy note
Out of a sound heart and a merry throat,
As if it said, "Good day, good sir.
Fine afternoon, old passenger!
Happy to meet you in these places
When January brings new faces!"

RALPH WALDO EMERSON

Four Ducks on a Pond

Four ducks on a pond,
A grass-bank beyond,
A blue sky of spring,
White clouds on the wing—
What a little thing
To remember for years!
To remember with tears!

WILLIAM ALLINGHAM

Dove

I had a dove, and the sweet dove died;
   And I have thought it died of grieving:
O, what could it grieve for? its feet were tied
   With a single thread of my own hand's weaving,
Sweet little red feet, why should you die—
Why should you leave me, sweet bird, why?
You lived alone in the forest tree,
Why, pretty thing! would you not live with me?
I kiss'd you oft and gave you white peas;
Why not live sweetly, as in the green trees?

JOHN KEATS

Answer to a Child's Question

Do you ask what the birds say? The Sparrow, the
   Dove,
The Linnet and Thrush say, "I love and I love!"
In the winter they're silent—the wind is so strong;
What it says, I don't know, but it sings a loud song.
But green leaves, and blossoms, and sunny warm
   weather.
And singing, and loving—all come back together.
But the Lark is so brimful of gladness and love,
The green fields below him, the blue sky above,
That he sings, and he sings; and for ever sings he—
"I love my Love, and my Love loves me!"

SAMUEL TAYLOR COLERIDGE

The Blackbird

The nightingale has a lyre of gold,
The lark's is a clarion call,
And the blackbird plays but a boxwood flute,
But I love him best of all.

For his song is all of the joy of life,
And we in the mad, spring weather,
We two have listened till he sang
Our hearts and lips together.

W. E. HENLEY

The Flight of Birds

The crow goes flopping on from wood to wood.
The wild duck wherries to the distant flood,
The starnels hurry o'er in merry crowds,
And overhead whew by like hasty clouds;
The wild duck from the meadow-water plies
And dashes up the water as he flies;
The pigeon suthers by on rapid wing,
The lark mounts upward at the call of spring.
In easy flights above the hurricane
With doubled neck high sails the noisy crane.
Whizz goes the pewit o'er the plowman's team,
With many a whew and whirl and sudden scream;
And lightly fluttering to the tree just by,
In chattering journeys whirls the noisy pie;
From bush to bush slow swees the screaming jay,
With one harsh note of pleasure all the day.

JOHN CLARE

The Owl

When cats run home and light is come,
　　And dew is cold upon the ground,
And the far-off stream is dumb,
　　And the whirring sail goes round,
　　And the whirring sail goes round;
　　　Alone and warming his five wits,
　　　The white owl in the belfry sits.

When merry milkmaids click the latch,
　　And rarely smells the new-mown hay,
And the cock hath sung beneath the thatch
　　Twice or thrice his roundelay,
　　Twice or thrice his roundelay;
　　　Alone and warming his five wits,
　　　The white owl in the belfry sits.

ALFRED, LORD TENNYSON

The Eagle

He clasps the crag with crooked hands;
Close to the sun in lonely lands,
Ring'd with the azure world, he stands,

The wrinkled sea beneath him crawls;
He watches from his mountain walls,
And like a thunderbolt he falls.

ALFRED, LORD TENNYSON

The Secret

We have a secret, just we three,
The robin, and I, and the sweet cherry-tree;
The bird told the tree, and the tree told me,
And nobody knows it but just us three.

But of course the robin knows it best,
Because he built the—I shan't tell the rest;
And laid the four little—something in it—
I'm afraid I shall tell it every minute.

But if the tree and the robin don't peep,
I'll try my best the secret to keep;
Though I know when the little birds fly about
Then the whole secret will be out.

EMILY DICKINSON

To an Oriole

How falls it, oriole, thou hast come to fly
In tropic splendor through our Northern sky?

At some glad moment was it nature's choice
To dower a scrap of sunset with a voice?

Or did some orange tulip, flaked with black,
In some forgotten garden, ages back,

Yearning toward Heaven until its wish was heard,
Desire unspeakably to be a bird?

EDGAR FAWCETT

The Horned Owl

In the hollow tree, in the old gray tower,
　　The spectral owl doth dwell;
Dull, hated, despised, in the sunshine hour,
　　But at dusk he's abroad and well!
Not a bird of the forest e'er mates with him;
　　All mock him outright by day;
But at night, when the woods grow still and dim,
　　The boldest will shrink away!
　　　O, *when the night falls, and roosts the fowls,*
　　Then, then, is the joy of the hornèd owl!

And the owl hath a bride, who is fond and bold,
　　And loveth the wood's deep gloom;
And with eyes like the shine of the moonstone cold,
　　She awaiteth her ghastly groom;
Not a feather she moves, not a carol she sings,
　　As she waits in her tree so still;
But when her heart heareth his flapping wings,
　　She hoots out her welcome shrill!
　　　O, *when the moon shines, and dogs do howl,*
　　Then, then, is the joy of the hornèd owl!

Mourn not for the owl, nor his gloomy plight!
　　The owl hath his share of good:
If a prisoner he be in the broad daylight,
　　He is lord in the dark greenwood!
Nor lonely the bird, nor his ghastly mate,
　　They are each unto each a pride;
Thrice fonder, perhaps, since a strange, dark fate
　　Hath rent them from all beside!
So, when the night falls, and dogs do howl,
Sing, ho! for the reign of the hornèd owl!
　　We know not alway who are kings by day,
But the king of the night is the bold brown owl!

BARRY CORNWALL

34

Skylark and Nightingale

When a mounting skylark sings
  In the sunlit summer morn,
I know that heaven is up on high,
  And on earth are fields of corn.

But when a nightingale sings
  In the moonlit summer even,
I know not if earth is merely earth,
  Only that heaven is heaven.

CHRISTINA ROSSETTI

To a Skylark

Hail to thee, blithe Spirit!
  Bird thou never wert,
That from heaven, or near it,
  Pourest thy full heart
In profuse strains of unpremeditated art.

Higher still and higher
  From the earth thou springest
Like a cloud of fire;
  The blue deep thou wingest.
And singing still dost soar, and soaring ever singest.

PERCY BYSSHE SHELLEY

The Lark

Hark! hark! the lark at heaven's gate sings,
  And Phoebus gins arise,
His steeds to water at those springs
  On chaliced flowers that lies;
And winking Mary-buds begin
  To ope their golden eyes;
With every thing that pretty is,
  My lady sweet, arise;
    Arise, arise!

WILLIAM SHAKESPEARE

Forbearance

Hast thou named all the birds without a gun?
Loved the wood-rose, and left it on its stalk?
At rich men's tables eaten bread and pulse?
Unarmed, faced danger with a heart of trust?
And loved so well a high behavior,
In man or maid, that thou from speech refrained,
Nobility more nobly to repay?
O, be my friend, and teach me to be thine!

RALPH WALDO EMERSON

To the Skylark

Ethereal minstrel! pilgrim of the sky!
Dost thou despise the earth where cares abound?
Or while the wings aspire, are heart and eye
Both with thy nest upon the dewy ground?
Thy nest which thou canst drop into at will,
Those quivering wings composed, that music still!

WILLIAM WORDSWORTH

Creatures Great and Small

The year's at the spring,
And day's at the morn;
Morning's at seven;
The hill-side's dew-pearled;
The lark's on the wing;
The snail's on the thorn;
God's in His Heaven—
All's right with the world!

ROBERT BROWNING

Hopping Frog

Hopping frog, hop here and be seen,
  I'll not pelt you with stick or stone:
Your cap is laced and your coat is green;
  Good-bye, we'll let each other alone.

Plodding toad, plod here and be looked at,
You the finger of scorn is crooked at:
But though you're lumpish, you're harmless too;
You won't hurt me, and I won't hurt you.

CHRISTINA ROSSETTI

The Toad and the Frog

"Croak!" said the Toad, "I'm hungry, I think;
Today I've had nothing to eat or to drink;
I'll crawl to a garden and jump through the pales,
And there I'll dine nicely on slugs and on snails."

"Ho, ho!" quoth the Frog, "is that what you mean?
Then I'll hop away to the next meadow stream;
There I will drink, and eat worms and slugs, too,
And then I shall have a good dinner like you."

38

King of Beasts

The Lion ramps around the cage,
The Lady smiles to see him rage.
The little Mouse outside the bars
Looks on and laughs. "Well, bless my stars!"
Quoth he, "to think they call that thing
The *King of Beasts!* If *he's* a King,
Who cannot make the Lady wince,
What must *I* be? When, not long since,
Inside the cage I chanced to slip.
You should have seen that Lady skip
Upon the Lion's back. 'Help! Murder!
A Mouse!' she screamed; you should have heard
  her!
And then with brooms the keepers came
And drove me out (but, all the same,
I got the crumb that I was after).
A King indeed! Excuse my laughter!"

OLIVER HERFORD

                   ✂

The beetle loves his unpretending track,
The snail the house he carries on his back;
The farfetched worm with pleasure would disown
The bed we give him, though of softest down.

WILLIAM WORDSWORTH

                   ✂

The Snail's Dream

A snail who had a way, it seems,
Of dreaming very curious dreams,
Once dream't he was—you'll never guess!—
The Lightning Limited Express!

OLIVER HERFORD

                   ✂

An Explanation of the Grasshopper

The Grasshopper, the Grasshopper,
I will explain to you:—
He is the Brownies' racehorse,
The Fairies' Kangaroo.

VACHEL LINDSAY

Pedigree

The pedigree of honey
Does not concern the bee;
A clover, any time, to him
Is aristocracy.

EMILY DICKINSON

                   ✂

The Caterpillar

Brown and furry
Caterpillar in a hurry,
Take your walk
To the shady leaf, or stalk,
  Or what not,
Which may be the chosen spot.
  No toad spy you,
Hovering bird of prey pass by you,
Spin and die,
To live again a butterfly.

CHRISTINA ROSSETTI

39

The City Mouse and the Garden Mouse

The city mouse lives in a house;—
   The garden mouse lives in a bower,
He's friendly with the frogs and toads,
   And sees the pretty plants in flower.

The city mouse eats bread and cheese;—
   The garden mouse eats what he can;
We will not grudge him seeds and stocks,
   Poor little timid furry man.

CHRISTINA ROSSETTI

The Kitten Speaks

I am the Cat of Cats. I am
   The everlasting cat!
Cunning, and old, and sleek as jam,
   The everlasting cat!
I hunt the vermin in the night—
   The everlasting cat!
For I see best without the light—
   The everlasting cat!

WILLIAM BRIGHTY RANDS

The Field Mouse

When the moon shines o'er the corn
And the beetle drones his horn,
And the flittermice swift fly,
And the nightjars swooping cry,
And the young hares run and leap,
We waken from our sleep.

And we climb with tiny feet
And we munch the green corn sweet
With startled eyes for fear
The white owl should fly near,
Or long slim weasel spring
Upon us where we swing.

We do not hurt at all;
Is there not room for all
Within the happy world?

All day we lie close curled
In drowsy sleep, nor rise
Til through the dusky skies
The moon shines o'er the corn
And the beetle drones his horn.

WILLIAM SHARP

A Kitten's Thought

It's very nice to think of how
In every country lives a Cow
To furnish milk with all her might
For Kitten's comfort and delight.

OLIVER HERFORD

Cats

"Pussy-cat, pussy-cat, where have you been?"
"I have been up to London to look at the Queen."
"Pussy-cat, pussy-cat, what did you there?"
"I frightened a little mouse under the chair."

The Drummer

Rat-a-tat-tat . . .
See Bunny come
Sporting green breeches
And rolling his drum.

Rat-a-tat-tat . . .
Little pink nose
Must have been snooping
Into a rose.

Rat-a-tat-tat . . .
Rabbit, the drummer,
Straightens his ears
And marches with summer.

ANNE ROBINSON

Clover

Little masters, hat in hand
Let me in your presence stand,
Till your silence solve for me
This your threefold mystery.

Tell me—for I long to know—
How, in darkness there below,
Was your fairy fabric spun,
Spread and fashioned, three in one.

Did your gossips gold and blue,
Sky and Sunshine, choose for you,
Ere your triple forms were seen,
Suited liveries of green?

Can ye,—if ye dwelt indeed
Captives of a prison seed,—
Like the Genie, once again
Get you back into the grain?

Little masters, may I stand
In your presence, hat in hand,
Waiting till you solve for me
This your threefold mystery?

JOHN BANISTER TABB

The Brook

I come from haunts of coot and hern,
  I make a sudden sally
And sparkle out among the fern,
  To bicker down a valley.

By thirty hills I hurry down,
  Or slip between the ridges,
By twenty thorps, a little town,
  And half a hundred bridges.

Till last by Philip's farm I flow
  To join the brimming river,
For men may come and men may go,
  But I go on for ever.

I chatter over stony ways,
  In little sharps and trebles,
I bubble into eddying bays,
  I babble on the pebbles.

With many a curve my banks I fret
  By many a field and fallow,
And many a fairy foreland set
  With willow-weed and mallow.

I chatter, chatter, as I flow
  To join the brimming river,
For men may come and men may go,
  But I go on for ever.

I wind about, and in and out,
  With here a blossom sailing,
And here and there a lusty trout,
  And here and there a grayling,

And here and there a foamy flake
  Upon me, as I travel
With many a silvery waterbreak
  Above the golden gravel.

I steal by lawns and grassy plots,
  I slide by hazel covers;
I move the sweet forget-me-nots
  That grow for happy lovers.

I slip, I slide, I gloom, I glance,
  Among my skimming swallows;
I make the netted sunbeam dance
  Against my sandy shallows.

I murmur under moon and stars
  In brambly wildernesses;
I linger by my shingly bars;
  I loiter round my cresses;

And out again I curve and flow
  To join the brimming river,
For men may come and men may go,
  But I go on for ever.

ALFRED, LORD TENNYSON

Mirror for Myself

Little squirrel
In the tree,
Are you not
Much like me?

Underneath the laughing sun,
    Hopping bold,
    You frisk and play;

But when rain and thunder come,
    Sulk and scold
    All the day.

ROGER WESCOTT

✦✦✦

The Squirrel

Whisky Frisky,
Hippity hop,
Up he goes
To the tree top!

Whiriy, twirly,
Round and round,
Down he scampers
To the ground.

Furly, curly,
What a tail!
Tall as a feather,
Broad as a sail!

Experiment to me
Is every one I meet.
If it contain a kernel?
The figure of a nut

Presents upon a tree,
Equally plausibly;
But meat within is requisite,
To squirrels and to me.

EMILY DICKINSON

✦✦✦

To a Squirrel

Come play with me;
Why should you run
Through the shaking tree
As though I'd a gun
To strike you dead?
When all I would do
Is to scratch your head
And let you go.

WILLIAM BUTLER YEATS

The Pony

I had a little pony,
   His name was Dapple-gray;
I lent him to a lady
   To ride a mile away.

She whipped him, she slashed him,
   She rode him through the mire.
I would not lend my pony now
   For all the lady's hire.

Horses

The horses of the sea
   Rear a foaming crest,
But the horses of the land
   Serve us best.

The horses of the land
   Munch corn and clover,
While the foaming sea-horses
   Toss and turn over.

CHRISTINA ROSSETTI

Colts

Colts behind their mothers
Trot across the plain,
Rustling, zoro-zoro, like a lady's train.

JAPANESE HOKKU

Say This of Horses

Across the ages they come thundering
  On faithful hoofs, the horses man disowns.
Their velvet eyes are wide with wondering;
  They whinny down the wind in silver tones
Vibrant with all the bugles of old wars;
  Their nostrils quiver with the summer scent
Of grasses in deep fields lit by pale stars
  Hung in a wide and silent firmament.
And in their hearts they keep the dreams of earth
  Their patient plodding furrowed to the sun
Unnumbered springs before the engine's birth
  Doomed them to sadness and oblivion.
Across the swift new day I watch them go
  Driven by wheel and gear and dynamo.

Say this of horses: engines leave behind
  No glorious legacy of waving manes
And wild proud hearts, and heels before the wind.
  No heritage of ancient Arab strains
Blazes within a cylinder's cold spark;
  An engine labors with a sullen fire,
Hoarding no dreams of acres sweet and dark:
  No love for man has ever surged through wire!
Along the farthest slopes I hear the rumble
  Of these last hoofs—tomorrow they will be still;
Then shall the stength of countless horses crumble
  The staunchest rock and level the highest hill;
And man who made machines to gain an hour
  Shall lose himself before their ruthless power.

MINNIE HITE MOODY

45

How Doth the Little Crocodile

How doth the little crocodile
   Improve his shining tail,
And pour the waters of the Nile
   On every golden scale!

How cheerfully he seems to grin,
   How neatly spreads his claws,
And welcomes little fishes in,
   With gently smiling jaws!

LEWIS CARROLL

The Secret

A fuzzy fellow without feet
Yet doth exceeding run!
Of velvet is his countenance
And his complexion dun.

Sometimes he dwelleth in the grass,
Sometimes upon a bough
From which he doth descend in plush
Upon the passer-by.

All this in summer—but when winds
Alarm the forest folk,
He taketh damask residence
And struts in sewing silk.

Then, finer than a lady,
Emerges in the spring,
A feather on each shoulder—
You'd scarce accredit him.

By men yclept a caterpillar—
By me—But who am I
To tell the pretty secret
Of the butterfly!

EMILY DICKINSON

The Kitten and the Falling Leaves

See the kitten on the wall,
Sporting with the leaves that fall,
Withered leaves—one—two—and three—
From the lofty elder-tree!
Through the calm and frosty air
Of this morning bright and fair,
Eddying round and round they sink
Softly, slowly: one might think
From the motions that are made,
Every little leaf conveyed
Sylph or fairy hither tending,
To this lower world descending,
Each invisible and mute,
In his wavering parachute.
—But the kitten, how she starts,
Crouches, stretches, paws and darts
First at one, and then its fellow,
Just as light and just as yellow!
Where are many now—now one—
Now they stop and there are none:
What intenseness of desire
In her upward eye of fire!
With a tiger-leap half-way
Now she meets the coming prey,
Lets it go as fast, and then
Has it in her power again:
Now she works with three or four,
Like an Indian conjurer;
Quick as he in feats of art,
Far beyond in joy of heart.
Were her antics played in the eye
Of a thousand standers-by,
Clapping hands with shouts and stare,
What would little Tabby care
For the plaudits of the crowd?
Over-happy to be proud,
Over-wealthy in the treasure
Of her own exceeding pleasure.

WILLIAM WORDSWORTH

46

The Stallion

A gigantic beauty of a stallion, fresh and responsive
   to my caresses.
Head high in the forehead, wide between the ears,
Limbs glossy·and supple, tail dusting the ground,
Eyes full of sparkling wickedness, ears finely cut,
   flexibly moving.
His nostrils dilate as my heels embrace him,
His well-built limbs tremble with pleasure as we
   race around and return.

WALT WHITMAN

The Horse

I will not change my horse with any that treads . . .
When I bestride him, I soar, I am a hawk.
He trots the air; the earth sings when he touches
   it.
The barest horn of his hoof is more musical than
   the pipe of Hermes . . .
He's of the color of the nutmeg and of the heat of
   the ginger . . .
He is pure air and fire, and the dull elements
Of earth and water never appear in him,
But only in patient stillness his rider mounts him. . .
It is the prince of palfreys. His neigh is like
The bidding of a monarch, and his countenance
Enforces homage.

WILLIAM SHAKESPEARE

47

Dance of Burros

Nothing at all more delicate and charming
than the way the donkeys came,
their eyes downcast like eyes of señoritas
taught to dissemble shame

their small hooves treading neatly, shoes of dancers
making a shape for music, striking the stones
into sudden tune, tapping the brookbed street
to echo on the adobe. How could bones

travel so nimbly under the tall sun
carrying burdens as the donkeys did:
curbed fields of cornstalks? And the pale maize
    rustled
in frail percussion from the carrying tread.

Piano piano piano the beasts drummed by
with delicate beat, as light as twigs on rile,
through raining light above their own small
    shadows
trotting in single file.

And three brown men in white, beneath sombreros,
moved with the donkeys quietly, to climb
the cobbled hill. The white walls yawned them in,
burros and men and burdens keeping time.

DILYS LAING

48

The Fly

Little Fly,
Thy summer's play
My thoughtless hand
Has brushed away.

Am not I
A fly like thee?
Or art not thou
A man like me?

For I dance,
And drink, and sing,
Till some blind hand
Shall brush my wing.

If thought is life
And strength and breath,
And the want
Of thought is death;

Then am I
A happy fly,
If I live
Or if I die.

WILLIAM BLAKE

*

Honey-Bees

They have a king and officers of sorts;
Where some, like magistrates, correct at home,
Others, like merchants, venture trade abroad,
Others, like soldiers, armed in their stings,
Make boot upon the summer's velvet buds,
Which pillage they with merry march bring home
To the tent-royal of their emperor;
Who, busied in his majesty, surveys
The singing masons building roofs of gold,
The civil citizens kneading up the honey,
The poor mechanic porters crowding in
Their heavy burdens at his narrow gate,
The sad-eyed justice, with his surly hum,
Delivering o'er to executors pale
The lazy yawning drone.

WILLIAM SHAKESPEARE

The Grasshopper and the Cricket

Green little vaulter in the sunny grass,
Catching your heart up at the feel of June,
Sole voice that's heard amidst the lazy noon,
When even the bees lag at the summoning brass;
And you, warm little housekeeper, who class
With those who think the candles come too soon,
Loving the fire, and with your tricksome tune
Nick the glad silent moments as they pass;

Oh sweet and tiny cousins, that belong,
One to the fields, the other to the hearth,
Both have your sunshine; both though small are
    strong
At your clear hearts; and both seem given to earth
To ring in thoughtful ears this natural song—
Indoors and out, summer and winter, Mirth.

LEIGH HUNT

Butterflies

There will be butterflies,
There will be summer skies
And flowers upthrust,
When all that Caesar bids,
And all the pyramids
    Are dust.

There will be gaudy wings
Over the bones of things,
And never grief:
Who says that summer skies,
Who says that butterflies,
    Are brief?

HANIEL LONG

White Butterflies

Fly, white butterflies, out to sea,
Frail, pale wings for the wind to try,
Small white wings that we scarce can see,
    Fly!
Some fly light as a laugh of glee,
Some fly soft as a long, low sigh;
All to the haven where each would be,
    Fly!

ALGERNON CHARLES SWINBURNE

Clock-a-clay

In the cowslip pips I lie,
Hidden from the buzzing fly,
While green grass beneath me lies,
Pearled with dew like fishes' eyes,
Here I lie, a clock-a-clay,
Waiting for the time of day.

While grassy forest quakes surprise,
And the wild wind sobs and sighs,
My gold home rocks as like to fall,
On its pillar green and tall;
When the pattering rain drives by
Clock-a-clay keeps warm and dry.

Day by day and night by night,
All the week I hide from sight;
In the cowslip pips I lie,
In rain and dew still warm and dry;
Day and night, and night and day,
Red, black-spotted clock-a-clay.

My home shakes in wind and showers,
Pale green pillar topped with flowers,
Bending at the wild wind's breath,
'Till I touch the grass beneath;
Here I live, lone clock-a-clay,
Watching for the time of day.

JOHN CLARE

The Little Turtle

There was a little turtle.
  He lived in a box.
He swam in a puddle.
  He climbed on the rocks.

He snapped at a mosquito.
  He snapped at a flea.
He snapped at a minnow.
  And he snapped at me.

He caught the mosquito.
  He caught the flea.
He caught the minnow.
  But he didn't catch me.

VACHEL LINDSAY

Lady-Bug

Lady-bug, lady-bug,
  Fly away home,
Your house is on fire,
  Your children will burn.
All but one
  And her name is Ann,
And she crept under
  The frying-pan.

The Flower-fed Buffaloes

The flower-fed buffaloes of the spring
In the days of long ago,
Ranged where the locomotives sing
And the prairie flowers lie low:
The tossing, blooming, perfumed grass
Is swept away by the wheat,
Wheels and wheels and wheels spin by
In the spring that still is sweet.
But the flower-fed buffaloes of the spring
Left us, long ago.
They gore no more, they bellow no more,
They trundle around the hills no more:
With the Blackfeet, lying low,
With the Pawnees, lying low,
Lying low.

VACHEL LINSDAY

Buffalo Dusk

The buffaloes are gone.
And those who saw the buffaloes are gone.
Those who saw the buffaloes by thousands and
how they pawed the prairie sod into dust with
their great hoofs, their great heads down
pawing on in a great pageant of dusk,
Those who saw the buffaloes are gone.
And the buffaloes are gone.

CARL SANDBURG

Splinter

The voice of the last cricket
across the first frost
is one kind of good-by.
It is so thin a splinter of singing.

CARL SANDBURG

The Tiger

Tiger! Tiger! burning bright
In the forests of the night,
What immortal hand or eye
Could frame thy fearful symmetry?

In what distant deeps or skies
Burnt the fire of thine eyes?
On what wings dare he aspire?
What the hand dare seize the fire?

And what shoulder, and what art,
Could twist the sinews of thy heart?
And when thy heart began to beat,
What dread hand? and what dread feet?

What the hammer? what the chain?
In what furnace was thy brain?
What the anvil? what dread grasp
Dare its deadly terrors clasp?

When the stars threw down their spears,
And water'd heaven with their tears,
Did he smile his work to see?
Did he who made the Lamb make thee?

Tiger! Tiger! burning bright
In the forests of the night,
What immortal hand or eye,
Dare frame thy fearful symmetry?

WILLIAM BLAKE

✺✺✺

The Blind Men and the Elephant

It was six men of Indostan,
    To learning much inclined,
Who went to see the Elephant
    (Though all of them were blind),
That each by observation
    Might satisfy his mind.

The First approached the Elephant,
    And happening to fall
Against his broad and sturdy side,
    At once began to bawl:
"God bless me! but the Elephant
    Is very like a wall!"

The Second, feeling of the tusk,
    Cried, "Ho! what have we here
So very round and smooth and sharp?
    To me 'tis mighty clear
This wonder of an Elephant
    Is very like a spear!"

The Third approached the animal,
    And happening to take
The squirming trunk within his hands,
    Thus boldly up and spake:
"I see," quoth he, "the Elephant
    Is very like a snake!"

The Fourth reached out his eager hand,
    And felt about the knee.
"What most this wondrous beast is like,
    Is mighty plain," quoth he;
" 'Tis clear enough the Elephant
    'Is very like a tree!"

The Fifth, who chanced to touch the ear,
    Said: "E'en the blindest man
Can tell what this resembles most;
    Deny the fact who can,
This marvel of an Elephant
    Is very like a fan!"

The Sixth no sooner had begun
    About the beast to grope,
Than, seizing on the swinging tail
    That fell within his scope,
"I see," quoth he, "the Elephant
    Is very like a rope!"

And so these men of Indostan
    Disputed loud and long,
Each in his own opinion
    Exceeding stiff and strong,
Though each was partly in the right,
    And all were in the wrong!

JOHN GODFREY SAXE

✺✺✺

Carnival and Fancy

I met a little Elf-man, once,
  Down where the lilies blow.
I asked him why he was so small,
  And why he didn't grow.

He slightly frowned, and with his eye
  He looked me through and through.
"I'm quite as big for me," said he,
  "As you are big for you."

JOHN KENDRICK BANGS

Merry-Go-Round

Purple horses with orange manes,
  Elephants pink and blue,
Tigers and lions that never were seen
  In circus parade or zoo!
Bring out your money and choose your steed,
  And prance to delightsome sound.
What fun if the world would turn some day
  Into a Merry-Go-Round!

RACHEL FIELD

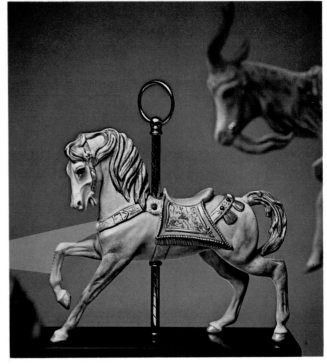

How to Tell the Wild Animals

If ever you should go by chance
   To jungles in the East;
And if there should to you advance
   A large and tawny beast,
If he roars at you as you're dyin'
You'll know it is the Asian Lion.

Or if sometime when roaming round,
   A noble wild beast greets you,
With black stripes on a yellow ground,
   Just notice if he eats you.
This simple rule may help you learn
The Bengal Tiger to discern.

If strolling forth, a beast you view,
   Whose hide with spots is peppered,
As soon as he has lept on you,
   You'll know it is the Leopard.
'Twill do no good to roar with pain,
He'll only lep and lep again.

If when you're walking round your yard,
   You meet a creature there,
Who hugs you very, very hard,
   Be sure it is the Bear.
If you have any doubt, I guess
He'll give you just one more caress.

Though to distinguish beasts of prey
   A novice might nonplus,
The Crocodiles you always may
   Tell from Hyenas thus:
Hyenas come with merry smiles;
But if they weep, they're Crocodiles.

The true Chameleon is small,
   A lizard sort of thing;
He hasn't any ears at all,
   And not a single wing.
If there is nothing on the tree,
'Tis the Chameleon you see.

CAROLYN WELLS

The Fairies

Up the airy mountain,
   Down the rushy glen,
We daren't go a-hunting
   For fear of little men;
Wee folk, good folk,
   Trooping all together;
Green jacket, red cap,
   And white owl's feather!

Down along the rocky shore
   Some make their home;
They live on crispy pancakes
   Of yellow tide-foam;
Some in the reeds
   Of the black mountain lake,
With frogs for their watch-dogs,
   All night awake.

High on the hill-top
   The old King sits;
He is now so old and grey
   He's nigh lost his wits.
With a bridge of white mist
   Columbkill he crosses,
On his stately journeys
   From Slieveleague to Rosses;
Or going up with music
   On cold starry nights,
To sup with the Queen
   Of the gay Northern Lights.

They stole little Bridget
   For seven years long;
When she came down again,
   Her friends were all gone.
They took her lightly back,
   Between the night and morrow,
They thought that she was fast asleep,
   But she was dead with sorrow.
They have kept her ever since
   Deep within the lake,
On a bed of flag-leaves,
   Watching till she wake.

By the craggy hill-side,
   Through the mosses bare,
They have planted thorn-trees
   For pleasure here and there.
Is any man so daring
   As dig them up in spite,
He shall find the thornies set
   In his bed at night.

Up the airy mountain,
   Down the rushy glen,
We daren't go a-hunting
   For fear of little men;
Wee folk, good folk,
   Trooping all together;
Green jacket, red cap,
   And white owl's feather!

WILLIAM ALLINGHAM

A Night with a Wolf

High up on the lonely mountains,
   Where the wild men watched and waited;
Wolves in the forest, and bears in the bush,
   And I on my path belated.

The rain and the night together
   Came down, and the wind came after,
Bending the props of the pine-tree roof,
   And snapping many a rafter.

I crept along in the darkness,
   Stunned, and bruised, and blinded;
Crept to a fir with thick-set boughs,
   And a sheltering rock behind it.

There, from the blowing and raining,
   Crouching, I sought to hide me.
Something rustled; two green eyes shone;
   And a wolf lay down beside me!

His wet fur pressed against me;
   Each of us warmed the other;
Each of us felt, in the stormy dark,
   That beast and man were brother.

And when the falling forest
   No longer crashed in warning,
Each of us went from our hiding place
   Forth in the wild, wet morning.

BAYARD TAYLOR

A Fairy in Armor

He put his acorn helmet on;
It was plumed on the silk of the thistle down;
The corslet plate that guarded his breast
Was once the wild bee's golden vest;
His cloak, of a thousand mingled dyes,
Was formed of the wings of butterflies;
His shield was the shell of a lady-bug green,
Studs of gold on a ground of green;
And the quivering lance which he brandished
    bright,
Was the sting of a wasp he had slain in fight.
Swift he bestrode his fire-fly steed;
    He bared his blade of the bent-grass blue;
He drove his spurs of the cockle-seed,
    And away like a glance of thought he flew,
To skim the heavens, and follow far
The fiery trail of the rocket-star.

JOSEPH RODMAN DRAKE

Fairy Song

Over hill, over dale,
    Through bush, through brier,
Over park, over pale,
    Through flood, through fire.
    I do wander everywhere,
    Swifter than the moonè's sphere;
And I serve the fairy queen,
    To dew her orbs upon the green:
    The cowslips tall her pensioners be;
    In their gold coats spots you see;
    Those be rubies, fairy favors,
    In those freckles live their savors:
I must go seek some dew-drops here,
And hang a pearl in every cowslip's ear.

WILLIAM SHAKESPEARE

Music

Let me go where'er I will
I hear a sky-born music still:
It sounds from all things old,
It sounds from all things young;
From all that's fair, from all that's foul,
Peals out a cheerful song.
It is not only in the rose,
It is not only in the bird,
Not only where the rainbow glows,
Nor in the song of woman heard,
But in the darkest, meanest things
There always, always something sings.
'Tis not in the high stars alone,
Nor in the cups of budding flowers,
Nor in the redbreast's mellow tone,
Nor in the bow that smiles in showers,
But in the mud and scum of things
There always, always something sings.

RALPH WALDO EMERSON

Jabberwocky

'Twas brillig, and the slithy toves
    Did gyre and gimble in the wabe:
All mimsy were the borogoves,
    And the mome raths outgrabe.

"Beware the Jabberwock, my son!
    The jaws that bite, the claws that catch!
Beware the Jubjub bird, and shun
    The frumious Bandersnatch!"

He took his vorpal sword in hand:
    Long time the manxome foe he sought—
So rested he by the Tumtum tree,
    And stood awhile in thought.

And, as in uffish thought he stood,
    The Jabberwock, with eyes of flame,
Came whiffling through the tulgey wood,
    And burbled as it came!

One, two! One, two! And through and through
    The vorpal blade went snicker-snack!
He left it dead, and with its head
    He went galumphing back.

"And hast thou slain the Jabberwock?
    Come to my arms, my beamish boy!
O frabjous day! Callooh! Callay!"
    He chortled in his joy.

'Twas brillig, and the slithy toves
    Did gyre and gimble in the wabe:
All mimsy were the borogoves,
    And the mome raths outgrabe.

LEWIS CARROLL

My Fairy Steed

O have you seen my fairy steed?
   His eyes are wild, his mane is white,
He feeds upon an elfin weed
   In cool of autumn night.

O have you heard my fairy steed,
   Whose cry is like a wandering loon?
He mourns some cloudy star-strewn mead
   On mountains of the moon.

O have you tamed my fairy horse
   To mount upon his back and ride?
He tears the great trees in his course,
   Nor ever turns aside.

'Tis he who tames a fairy thing,
   Must suffer want and bitter fate!
Deftly the bridles did I fling
   That brought him to my gate

I soothed and fed and tendered him
  Sweet herbs and honey in a cup,
And led him in the twilight dim
  To where a spring welled up.

But there his wings they waved so bright
  Before my eyes, I drooped and slept.
When I awoke, it seemed dark night.
  I raised my voice and wept.

Alas my lightsome fairy steed!
  I saw my pastures trampled bare
Where I had sown the springtime seed
  And planted flowers rare!

I saw my barns a mass of flame!
  His fiery wings had glanced in flight.
And me—a prey to fear and shame—
  He left, to seek the light!

LAURA BENÉT

The Unicorn

While yet the Morning Star
Flamed in the sky
A Unicorn went mincing by,
Whiter by far than blossom of the thorn:
His silver horn
Glittered as he danced and pranced
Silver-pale in the silver-pale morn.

The folk that saw him, ran away.
Where he went, so gay, so fleet,
Star-like lilies at his feet
Flowered all day,
Lilies, lilies in a throng,
And the wind made for him a song:

But he dared not stay
Over-long!

ELLA YOUNG

The Fly-Away Horse

Oh, a wonderful horse is the Fly-Away Horse—
  Perhaps you have seen him before;
Perhaps, while you slept, his shadow has swept
  Through the moonlight that floats on the floor.
For it's only at night, when the stars twinkle bright,
  That the Fly-Away Horse, with a neigh
And a pull at his rein and a toss of his mane,
  Is up on his heels and away!
    The Moon in the sky,
    As he gallopeth by,
  Cries: "Oh! what a marvelous sight!"
    And the Stars in dismay
    Hide their faces away
  In the lap of old Grandmother Night.

It is yonder, out yonder, the Fly-Away Horse
  Speedeth ever and ever away—
Over meadows and lanes, over mountains and plains,
  Over streamlets that sing at their play;
And over the sea like a ghost sweepeth he,
  While the ships they go sailing below,
And he speedeth so fast that the men at the mast
  Adjudge him some portent of woe.
    "What ho, there!" they cry,
    As he flourishes by
  With a whisk of his beautiful tail;
    And the fish in the sea
    Are as scared as can be,
  From the nautilus up to the whale!

And the Fly-Away Horse seeks those far-away lands
  You little folk dream of at night—
Where candy-trees grow, and honey-brooks flow,
  And corn-fields with popcorn are white;
And the beasts in the wood are ever so good
  To children who visit them there—
What glory astride of a lion to ride,
  Or to wrestle around with a bear!
    The monkeys, they say:
    "Come on, let us play,"
  And they frisk in the coconut-trees:
    While the parrots, that cling
    To the peanut-vines, sing
  Or converse with comparative ease!

Off! scamper to bed—you shall ride him to-night!
  For, as soon as you've fallen asleep,
With a jubilant neigh he shall bear you away

    Over forest and hillside and deep!
But tell us, my dear, all you see and you hear
  In those beautiful lands over there,
Where the Fly-Away Horse wings his far-away
  course
  With the wee one consigned to his care.
    Then grandma will cry
    In amazement: "Oh, my!"
  And she'll think it could never be so.
    And only we two
    Shall know it is true—
  You and I, little precious! shall know!

EUGENE FIELD

The Purple Cow

Reflections on a Mythic Beast,
Who's Quite Remarkable, at Least.

I never saw a Purple Cow,
I never Hope to See One.
But I can Tell You Anyhow,
I'd rather See than Be One.

GELETT BURGESS

Aladdin

When I was a beggarly boy,
  And lived in a cellar damp,
I had not a friend nor a toy,
  But I had Aladdin's lamp;
When I could not sleep for the cold,
  I had fire enough in my brain,
And builded, with roofs of gold,
  My beautiful castles in Spain!

Since then I have toiled day and night,
  I have money and power good store,
But I'd give all my lamps of silver bright
  For the one that is mine no more.
Take, Fortune, whatever you choose;
  You gave, and may snatch again;
I have nothing 'twould pain me to lose,
  For I own no more castles in Spain!

JAMES RUSSELL LOWELL

The Land of Story-books

He ate and drank the precious words,
His spirit grew robust;
He knew no more that he was poor,
Nor that his frame was dust.
He danced along the dingy days,
And this bequest of wings
Was but a book. What liberty
A loosened spirit brings!

EMILY DICKINSON

The Land of Story-books

At evening when the lamp is lit,
Around the fire my parents sit;
They sit at home and talk and sing
And do not play at anything.

Now, with my little gun, I crawl
All in the dark along the wall,
And follow round the forest track
Away behind the sofa back.

There, in the night, where none can spy,
All in my hunter's camp I lie,
And play at books that I have read
Till it is time to go to bed.

These are the hills, these are the woods,
These are my starry solitudes;
And there the river by whose brink
The roaring lions come to drink.

I see the others far away
As if in firelit camp they lay,
And I, like to an Indian scout,
Around their party prowled about.

So, when my nurse comes in for me,
Home I return across the sea,
And go to bed with backward looks
At my dear land of Story-books.

ROBERT LOUIS STEVENSON

The Children's Hour

Between the dark and the daylight,
    When the night is beginning to lower,
Comes a pause in the day's occupations,
    That is known as the Children's Hour.

I hear in the chamber above me
    The patter of little feet,
The sound of a door that is opened,
    And voices soft and sweet.

From my study I see in the lamplight,
    Descending the broad hall stair,
Grave Alice, and laughing Allegra,
    And Edith with golden hair.

A whisper, and then a silence:
    Yet I know by their merry eyes
They are plotting and planning together
    To take me by surprise.

A sudden rush from the stairway,
    A sudden raid from the hall!
By three doors left unguarded
    They enter my castle wall!

They climb up into my turret
    O'er the arms and back of my chair;
If I try to escape, they surround me;
    They seem to be everywhere.

They almost devour me with kisses,
    Their arms about me entwine,
Till I think of the Bishop of Bingen
    In his Mouse-Tower on the Rhine!

Do you think, O blue-eyed banditti,
    Because you have scaled the wall,
Such an old mustache as I am
    Is not a match for you all!

I have you fast in my fortress,
    And will not let you depart,
But put you down into the dungeon
    In the round-tower of my heart.

And there will I keep you forever,
    Yes, forever and a day,
Till the walls shall crumble to ruin,
    And moulder in dust away.

HENRY WADSWORTH LONGFELLOW

Birthdays

Monday's child is fair of face,
Tuesday's child is full of grace,
Wednesday's child is full of woe,
Thursday's child has far to go,
Friday's child is loving and giving,
Saturday's child works hard for its living;
But the child who is born on the Sabbath day
Is bonny and blithe and good and gay.

The Babes in the Wood

My dear, do you know
How a long time ago,
   Two poor little children,
Whose names I don't know,
Were stolen away
On a fine summer's day,
   And left in a wood,
As I've heard people say.

And when it was night,
So sad was their plight,
   The sun it went down,
And the moon gave no light!
They sobbed and they sighed,
And they bitterly cried,
   And the poor little things,
They lay down and died.

And when they were dead,
The robins so red
   Brought strawberry leaves
And over them spread;
And all the day long,
They sang them this song:—
   Poor babes in the wood!
   Poor babes in the wood!
And won't you remember
   The babes in the wood?

The Nut-Tree

I had a little nut-tree, nothing would it bear
But a silver nutmeg and a golden pear.

The king of Spain's daughter came to visit me,
And all because of my little nut-tree.

I skipped over water, I danced over sea,
And all the birds in the air couldn't catch me.

There Was a Little Girl

There was a little girl, she had a little curl
   Right in the middle of her forehead;
And when she was good, she was very, very good
   And when she was bad, she was horrid.

HENRY WADSWORTH LONGFELLOW

My Recollectest Thoughts

My recollectest thoughts are those
   Which I remember yet;
And bearing on, as you'd suppose,
   The things I don't forget.

But my resemblest thoughts are less
   Alike than they should be;
A state of things, as you'll confess,
   You very seldom see.

And yet the mostest thought I love
   Is what no one believes—
That I'm the sole survivor of
   The famous Forty Thieves!

CHARLES EDWARD CARRYL

The Naughty Boy

There was a naughty boy,
   And a naughty boy was he,
He ran away to Scotland
   The people for to see—
    Then he found
    That the ground
    Was as hard,
    That a yard
    Was as long,
    That a song
    Was as merry,
    That a cherry
    Was as red—
    That lead
    Was as weighty,
    That fourscore
    Was as eighty,
    That a door
    Was as wooden
    As in England—
So he stood in his shoes
   And he wondered,
   He wondered.
He stood in his shoes
   And he wondered.

JOHN KEATS

Little Buttercup

For I'm called Little Buttercup—dear Little
 Buttercup,
 Though I could never tell why,
But still I'm called Buttercup—poor Little
 Buttercup,
 Sweet Little Buttercup I!

I've snuff and tobaccy, and excellent jacky,
 I've scissors, and watches, and knives;
I've ribbons and laces to set off the faces
 Of pretty young sweethearts and wives.

I've treacle and toffee, I've tea and I've coffee,
 Soft tommy and succulent chops;
I've chickens and conies, and pretty polonies,
 And excellent peppermint drops.

Then buy of your Buttercup—dear Little
 Buttercup;
 Sailors should never be shy;
So, buy of your Buttercup—poor Little
 Buttercup;
 Come, of your Buttercup buy!

W. S. GILBERT

The Shepherdess

She walks—the lady of my delight—
 A shepherdess of sheep.
Her flocks are thoughts. She
 keeps them white;
 She guards them from the steep;
She feeds them on the fragrant height,
 And folds them in for sleep.

She roams maternal hills and bright,
 Dark valleys safe and deep.
Into that tender breast at night
 The chastest stars may peep.
She walks—the lady of my delight—
 A shepherdess of sheep.

She holds her little thoughts in sight,
 Though gay they run and leap.
She is so circumspect and right;
 She has her soul to keep.
She walks—the lady of my delight—
 A shepherdess of sheep.

ALICE MEYNELL

The Sugarplum Tree

Have you ever heard of the Sugarplum Tree?
   'Tis a marvel of great renown!
It blooms on the shore of the Lollipop Sea
   In the garden of Shut-Eye Town;
The fruit that it bears is so wondrously sweet
   (As those who have tasted it say)
That good little children have only to eat
   Of that fruit to be happy next day.

When you've got to the tree, you would have a
    hard time
   To capture the fruit which I sing;
The tree is so tall that no person could climb
   To the boughs where the sugarplums swing!
But up in that tree sits a chocolate cat,
   And a gingerbread dog prowls below—
And this is the way you contrive to get at
   Those sugarplums tempting you so:

You say but the word to that gingerbread dog
   And he barks with such terrible zest
That the chocolate cat is at once all agog,
   As her swelling proportions attest.
And the chocolate cat goes cavorting around
   From this leafy limb unto that,
And the sugarplums tumble, of course, to the
    ground—
   Hurrah for that chocolate cat!

There are marshmallows, gumdrops, and
    peppermint canes,
   With stripings of scarlet or gold,
And you carry away of the treasure that rains
   As much as your apron can hold!
So come, little child, cuddle closer to me
   In your dainty white nightcap and gown,
And I'll rock you away to that Sugarplum Tree
   In the garden of Shut-Eye Town.

EUGENE FIELD

The Reformation of Godfrey Gore

Godfrey Gordon Gustavus Gore—
No doubt you have heard the name before—
Was a boy who never would shut a door!

The wind might whistle, the wind might roar,
And teeth be aching and throats be sore,
But still he never would shut the door.

His father would beg, his mother implore,
"Godrey Gordon Gustavus Gore,
We really *do* wish you would shut the door!"

Their hands they wrung, their hair they tore;
But Godfrey Gordon Gustavus Gore
Was deaf as the buoy out at the Nore.

When he walked forth the folks would roar,
"Godfrey Gordon Gustavus Gore,
Why don't you think to shut the door?"

They rigged out a Shutter with sail and oar,
And threatened to pack off Gustavus Gore
On a voyage of penance to Singapore.

But he begged for mercy, and said, "No more!
Pray do not send me to Singapore
On a Shutter, and then I will shut the door!"

"You will?" said his parents; "then keep on shore!
But mind you do! For the plague is sore
Of a fellow that never will shut the door,
Godfrey Gordon Gustavus Gore!"

WILLIAM BRIGHTY RANDS

✤✤✤

The Owl and the Pussy-Cat

The Owl and the Pussy-Cat went to sea
    In a beautiful pea-green boat:
They took some honey, and plenty of money
    Wrapped up in a five-pound note.
The Owl looked up to the moon above,
    And sang to a small guitar,
"O lovely Pussy! O Pussy, my love!
    What a beautiful Pussy you are,—
        You are,
What a beautiful Pussy you are!"

Pussy said to the Owl, "You elegant fowl!
    How wonderful sweet you sing!
O let us be married,—too long we have tarried:—
    But what shall we do for a ring?"
They sailed away, for a year and a day
    To the land where the Bong-tree grows,
And there in a wood a piggy-wig stood,
    With a ring in the end of his nose,—
        His nose,
With a ring in the end of his nose.

"Dear Pig, are you willing to sell for one shilling
    Your ring?" Said the piggy, "I will."
So they took it away, and were married next day
    By the turkey who lives on the hill.
They dined upon mince and slices of quince,
    Which they ate with a runcible spoon;
And hand in hand, on the edge of the sand,
    They danced by the light of the moon,—
        The moon,
They danced by the light of the moon.

EDWARD LEAR

Wynken, Blynken, and Nod

Wynken, Blynken, and Nod one night
  Sailed off in a wooden shoe,—
Sailed on a river of crystal light
  Into a sea of dew.
"Where are you going, and what do you wish?"
  The old moon asked the three.
"We have come to fish for the herring fish
  That live in this beautiful sea;
Nets of silver and gold have we!"
      Said Wynken,
      Blynken,
      And Nod.

The old moon laughed and sang a song,
  As they rocked in the wooden shoe;
And the wind that sped them all night long
  Ruffled the waves of dew.
The little stars were the herring fish
  That lived in that beautiful sea—
"Now cast your nets wherever you wish,—
  Never afeard are we!"
So cried the stars to the fishermen three,
      Wynken,
      Blynken,
      And Nod.

All night long their nets they threw
  To the stars in the twinkling foam,—
Then down from the skies came the wooden shoe,
  Bringing the fishermen home:
'Twas all so pretty a sail, it seemed
  As if it could not be;
And some folk thought 'twas a dream they'd
    dream
  Of sailing that beautiful sea;
But I shall name you the fishermen three:
      Wynken,
      Blynken,
      And Nod.

Wynken and Blynken are two little eyes,
  And Nod is a little head,

And the wooden shoe that sailed the skies
  Is a wee one's trundle-bed;
So shut your eyes while Mother sings
  Of wonderful sights that be,
And you shall see the beautiful things
  As you rock in the misty sea
Where the old shoe rocked the fishermen three:—
      Wynken,
      Blynken,
      And Nod.

EUGENE FIELD

The Rock-a-By Lady

The Rock-a-By Lady from Hushaby Street
  Comes stealing; comes creeping;
The poppies they hang from her head to her feet,
And each hath a dream that is tiny and fleet—
She bringeth her poppies to you, my sweet,
  When she findeth you sleeping!

There is one little dream of a beautiful drum—
  "Rub-a-dub!" it goeth;
There is one little dream of a big sugar-plum,
And lo! thick and fast the other dreams come
Of popguns that bang, and tin tops that hum,
  And a trumpet that bloweth!

And dollies peep out of those wee little dreams
  With laughter and singing;
And boats go a-floating on silvery streams,
And the stars peek-a-boo with their own misty
    gleams,
And up, up, and up, where the Mother Moon
    beams,
  The fairies go winging!

Would you dream all these dreams that are tiny and
    fleet?
  They'll come to you sleeping;
So shut the two eyes that are weary, my sweet,
For the Rock-a-By Lady from Hushaby Street,
With poppies that hang from her head to her feet,
  Comes stealing; comes creeping.

EUGENE FIELD

The Duel

The gingham dog and the calico cat
Side by side on the table sat;
'Twas half past twelve, and (what do you think!)
Nor one nor t'other had slept a wink!
  The old Dutch clock and the Chinese plate
  Appeared to know as sure as fate
There was going to be a terrible spat.
    (I wasn't there: I simply state
    What was told to me by the Chinese plate!)

The gingham dog went, "Bow-wow-wow!"
And the calico cat replied, "Mee-ow!"
The air was littered, an hour or so,
With bits of gingham and calico,
  While the old Dutch clock in the chimney-place
  Up with its hands before its face,
  For it always dreaded a family row!
    (Now mind; I'm only telling you
    What the old Dutch clock declares is true!)

The Chinese plate looked very blue,
And wailed, "Oh, dear! what shall we do!"
But the gingham dog and calico cat
Wallowed this way and tumbled that,
  Employing every tooth and claw
  In the awfullest way you ever saw—
And, oh! how the gingham and calico flew!
    (Don't fancy I exaggerate—
    I got my news from the Chinese plate!)

Next morning, where the two had sat
They found no trace of dog or cat:
And some folks think unto this day
That burglars stole that pair away!
  But the truth about the cat and pup
  Is this: they ate each other up!
Now what do you really think of that!
    (The old Dutch clock it told me so,
    And that is how I came to know.)

EUGENE FIELD

Little Boy Blue

The little toy dog is covered with dust,
  But sturdy and stanch he stands;
And the little toy soldier is red with rust,
  And his musket moulds in his hands.

Time was when the little toy dog was new,
  And the soldier was passing fair;
And that was the time when our Little Boy Blue
  Kissed them and put them there.

"Now, don't you go till I come," he said,
  "And don't you make any noise!"
So, toddling off to his trundle-bed,
  He dreamt of the pretty toys;
And, as he was dreaming, an angel song
  Awakened our Little Boy Blue—
Oh! the years are many, the years are long,
  But the little toy friends are true!

Ay, faithful to Little Boy Blue they stand,
  Each in the same old place,
Awaiting the touch of a little hand,
  The smile of a little face;
And they wonder, as waiting the long years through
  In the dust of that little chair,
What has become of our Little Boy Blue,
  Since he kissed them and put them there.

EUGENE FIELD

What can Lambkins do?

  What can lambkins do
  All the keen night through?
Nestle by their woolly mother,
  The careful ewe.

  What can nestlings do
  In the nightly dew?
Sleep beneath their mother's wing
  Till day breaks anew.

  If in field or tree
  There might only be
Such a warm soft sleeping-place
  Found for me!

CHRISTINA ROSSETTI

I'm nobody! Who are you?
Are you nobody, too?
Then there's a pair of us—don't tell!
They'd banish us, you know.

How dreary to be somebody!
How public, like a frog
To tell your name the livelong day
To an admiring bog!

EMILY DICKINSON

If No One Ever Marries Me

If no one ever marries me—
And I don't see why they should,
For Nurse says I'm not pretty,
And I'm seldom very good—

If no one ever marries me
I shan't mind very much;
I shall buy a squirrel in a cage,
And a little rabbit-hutch.

I shall have a cottage near a wood,
And a pony all my own,
And a little lamb quite clean and tame
That I can take to town.

And when I'm getting *really* old—
At twenty-eight or nine—
I shall buy a little orphan girl,
And bring her up as mine.

(If no one ever marries me—
And I don't see why they should!)

LAURENCE ALMA-TADEMA

Sally in Our Alley

Of all the girls that are so smart
   There's none like pretty Sally;
She is the darling of my heart,
   And she lives in our alley.
There is no lady in the land
   Is half so sweet as Sally;
She is the darling of my heart,
   And she lives in our alley.

Her father he makes cabbage-nets
   And through the streets does cry 'em;
Her mother she sells laces long
   To such as please to buy 'em:
But sure such folks could ne'er beget
   So sweet a girl as Sally!
She is the darling of my heart,
   And she lives in our alley.

Of all the days that's in the week
   I dearly love but one day—
And that's the day that comes betwixt
   A Saturday and Monday;
For then I'm drest all in my best
   To walk abroad with Sally;
She is the darling of my heart,
   And she lives in our alley.

HENRY CAREY

The Village Blacksmith

Under a spreading chestnut-tree
  The village smithy stands;
The smith, a mighty man is he,
  With large and sinewy hands;
And the muscles of his brawny arms
  Are strong as iron bands.

His hair is crisp, and black, and long,
  His face is like the tan;
His brow is wet with honest sweat,
  He earns what'er he can,
And looks the whole world in the face,
  For he owes not any man.

Week in, week out, from morn till night,
  You can hear his bellows blow;
You can hear him swing his heavy sledge
  With measured beat and slow,
Like a sexton ringing the village bell,
  When the evening sun is low.

And children coming home from school
  Look in at the open door;
They love to see the flaming forge,
  And hear the bellows roar,
And catch the burning sparks that fly
  Like chaff from a threshing-floor.

He goes on Sunday to the church,
  And sits among his boys;
He hears the parson pray and preach,
  He hears his daughter's voice,
Singing in the village choir,
  And it makes his heart rejoice.

It sounds to him like her mother's voice,
  Singing in Paradise!
He needs must think of her once more,
  How in the grave she lies;
And with his hard, rough hand he wipes
  A tear out of his eyes.

Toiling,—rejoicing,—sorrowing,
  Onward through life he goes;
Each morning sees some task begin,
  Each evening sees it close;
Something attempted, something done,
  Has earned a night's repose.

Thanks, thanks to thee, my worthy friend,
  For the lesson thou has taught!
Thus at the flaming forge of life
  Our fortunes must be wrought;
Thus on its sounding anvil shaped
  Each burning deed and thought!

HENRY WADSWORTH LONGFELLOW

Whole Duty of Children

A child should always say what's true
And speak when he is spoken to,
And behave mannerly at table;
At least as far as he is able.

ROBERT LOUIS STEVENSON

The Oracle

I lay upon the summer grass.
  A gold-haired, sunny child came by,
And looked at me, as loath to pass,
  With questions in Her lingering eye.

She stopped and wavered, then drew near,
  (Ah! the pale gold around her head!)
And o'er my shoulder stopped to peer.
  "Why do you read?" she said.

"I read a poet of old time,
  Who sang through all his living hours—
Beauty of earth—the streams, the flowers—
  And stars, more lovely than his rhyme.

"And now I read him, since men go,
  Forgetful of these sweetest things;
Since he and I love brooks that flow,
  And dawns, and bees, and flash of wings!"

She stared at me with laughing look,
  Then clasped her hands upon my knees:
"How strange to read it in a book!
  I could have told you all of these!"

ARTHUR DAVISON FICKE

A Visit From St. Nicholas

'Twas the night before Christmas, when all
    through the house
Not a creature was stirring, not even a mouse;
The stockings were hung by the chimney with
    care,
In hopes that St. Nicholas soon would be there;
The children were nestled all snug in their beds,
While visions of sugar-plums danced in their
    heads;
And mamma in her kerchief, and I in my cap,
Had just settled our brains for a long winter nap,—
When out on the lawn there arose such a clatter,
I sprang from my bed to see what was the matter.
Away to the window I flew like a flash,
Tore open the shutters and threw up the sash.
The moon, on the breast of the new-fallen snow,
Gave a luster of midday to objects below;
When what to my wondering eyes should appear
But a miniature sleigh and eight tiny reindeer,
With a little old driver, so lively and quick,
I knew in a moment it must be St. Nick.
More rapid than eagles his coursers they came,
And he whistled, and shouted, and called them by
    name:
"Now, Dasher! now, Dancer! now, Prancer and
    Vixen!
On, Comet! On, Cupid! On, Dunder and Blixen!—
To the top of the porch! to the top of the wall!
Now, dash away, dash away, dash away all!"
As dry leaves that before the wild hurricane fly,
When they meet with an obstacle, mount to the
    sky,
So up to the house-top the coursers they flew,
With the sleigh full of toys—and St. Nicholas, too.
And then in a twinkling I heard on the roof
The prancing and pawing of each little hoof.
As I drew in my head, and was turning around,
Down the chimney St. Nicholas came with a
    bound.
He was dressed all in fur from his head to his foot,
And his clothes were all tarnished with ashes and
    soot,
A bundle of toys he had flung on his back,
And he looked like a peddler just opening his pack.
His eyes, how they twinkled! his dimples, how
    merry!
His cheeks were like roses, his nose like a cherry;

His droll little mouth was drawn up like a bow,
And the beard on his chin was as white as the
    snow.
The stump of a pipe he held tight in his teeth,
And the smoke, it encircled his head like a wreath.
He had a broad face and a little round belly
That shook, when he laughed, like a bowl full of
    jelly.
He was chubby and plump—a right jolly old elf;
And I laughed when I saw him, in spite of myself.
A wink of his eye, and a twist of his head,
Soon gave me to know I had nothing to dread.
He spoke not a word, but went straight to his
    work,
And filled all the stockings; then turned with a
    jerk,
And laying his finger aside of his nose,
And giving a nod, up the chimney he rose.
He sprang to his sleigh, to his team gave a whistle,
And away they all flew like the down of a thistle;
But I heard him exclaim, ere he drove out of sight,
"Happy Christmas to all, and to all a good-night!"

CLEMENT C. MOORE

∽∾∽

Christmas Everywhere

Everywhere, everywhere, Christmas to-night!
Christmas in lands of the fir tree and pine,
Christmas in lands of the palm tree and vine,
Christmas where snow peaks stand solemn and white,
Christmas where cornfields lie sunny and bright!

Christmas where children are hopeful and gay,
Christmas where old men are patient and gray,
Christmas where peace, like a dove in his flight,
Broods o'er brave men in the thick of the fight,
Everywhere, everywhere, Christmas to-night.

For the Christ Child who comes is the Master of all;
No palace too great and no cottage too small.

PHILLIPS BROOKS

The Quangle Wangle's Hat

On the top of the Crumpetty Tree
The Quangle Wangle sat,
But his face you could not see,
   On account of his Beaver Hat.
For his Hat was a hundred and two feet wide,
With ribbons and bibbons on every side,
And bells, and buttons, and loops, and lace,
So that nobody ever could see the face
     Of the Quangle Wangle Quee.

The Quangle Wangle said
   To himself on the Crumpetty Tree,
   "Jam, and jelly, and bread
    Are the best of food for me!
But the longer I live on this Crumpetty Tree
The plainer than ever it seems to me
That very few people come this way
And that life on the whole is far from gay!"
     Said the Quangle Wangle Quee.

But there came to the Crumpetty Tree
   Mr. and Mrs. Canary;
And they said, "Did ever you see
   Any spot so charmingly airy?
May we build a nest on your lovely Hat?
Mr. Quangle Wangle, grant us that!
O please let us come and build a nest
Of whatever material suits you best,
     Mr. Quangle Wangle Quee!"

And besides, to the Crumpetty Tree
   Came the Stork, the Duck, and the Owl;
The Snail and the Bumble-Bee,
   The Frog and the Fimble Fowl
(The Fimble Fowl, with a Corkscrew leg);
And all of them said, "We humbly beg
We may build our homes on your lovely Hat,—
Mr. Quangle Wangle, grant us that!
     Mr. Quangle Wangle Quee!"

And the Golden Grouse came there,
   And the Pobble who has no toes,
And the small Olympian bear,
   And the Dong with a luminous nose.
And the Blue Baboon who played the flute,

And the Orient Calf from the Land of Tute,
And the Attery Squash, and the Bisky Bat,—
All came and built on the lovely Hat
     Of the Quangle Wangle Quee.

And the Quangle Wangle said
   To himself on the Crumpetty Tree,
"When all these creatures move
   What a wonderful noise there'll be!"
And at night by the light of the Mulberry moon
They danced to the Flute of the Blue Baboon,
On the broad green leaves of the Crumpetty Tree,
And all were as happy as happy could be,
     With the Quangle Wangle Quee.

EDWARD LEAR

My Shadow

I have a little shadow that goes in and out with me,
And what can be the use of him is more than I can
   see.
He is very, very like me from the heels up to the
   head;
And I see him jump before me, when I jump into
   my bed.

The funniest thing about him is the way he likes
   to grow—
Not at all like proper children, which is always
   very slow;
For he sometimes shoots up taller like an India-
   rubber ball,
And he sometimes get so little that there's none of
   him at all.

He hasn't got a notion of how children ought to
   play,
And can only make a fool of me in every sort of
   way.
He stays so close beside me, he's a coward you can
   see;
I'd think shame to stick to nursie as that shadow
   sticks to me!

One morning, very early, before the sun was up,
I rose and found the shining dew on every
   buttercup;
But my lazy little shadow, like an arrant
   sleepyhead,
Had stayed at home behind me and was fast asleep
   in bed.

ROBERT LOUIS STEVENSON

The Day of the Circus Horse

It was a fiery circus horse
   That ramped and stamped and neighed
Till every creature in its course
   Fled, frightened and dismayed.

The chickens on the roadway's edge
   Arose and flapped their wings,
And making for the sheltering hedge
   Flew off like crazy things.

But when, at dusk, a little lame,
   It slowly climbed the stairs,
Behold! a gentle lady came
   And made it say its prayers.
Now, what a wondrous change you see!
   'Sh! Come and take a peep—
Here lies, as tame as tame can be,
   A little boy, asleep!

                    T. A. DALY

Yankee Doodle went to town
   Upon a little pony;
He stuck a feather in his hat
   And called it Macaroni.

Yankee Doodle

Father and I went down to camp,
Along with Cap'n Goodwin,
And there we saw the men and boys,
As thick as hasty puddin'!

Yankee Doodle, keep it up,
Yankee Doodle dandy,
Mind the music and the step,
And with the girls be handy!

And there we see a thousand men.
As rich as Squire David;
And what they wasted ev'ry day.
I wish it could be saved.

Chamber Music

Lean out of the window,
  Golden hair,
I hear you singing
  A merry air.

My book is closed;
  I read no more,
Watching the fire dance
  On the floor.

I have left my books:
  I have left my room:
For I heard you singing
  Through the gloom.

Singing and singing
  A merry air.
Lean out of the window,
  Golden hair.

JAMES JOYCE

75

The Battle of Blenheim

It was a summer's evening,
   Old Kaspar's work was done,
And he before his cottage door
   Was sitting in the sun;
And by him sported on the green
His little grandchild Wilhelmine.

She saw her brother Peterkin
   Roll something large and round,
Which he, beside the rivulet,
   In playing there, had found.
He came to ask what he had found,
That was so large, and smooth, and round.

Old Kaspar took it from the boy,
   Who stood expectant by;
And then the old man shook his head,
   And, with a natural sigh,
" 'Tis some poor fellow's skull," said he,
"Who fell in the great victory!

"I find them in the garden,
   For there's many here about;
And often when I go to plough,
   The ploughshare turns them out;
For many thousand men," said he,
"Were slain in that great victory!"

"Now tell us what 'twas all about,"
   Young Peterkin he cries;
And little Wilhelmine looks up
   With wonder-waiting eyes;
"Now tell us all about the war,
And what they fought each other for."

"It was the English," Kaspar cried,
   "Who put the French to rout;
But what they fought each other for
   I could not well make out;
But everybody said," quoth he,
"That 'twas a famous victory!

"My father lived at Blenheim then,
   Yon little stream hard by.
They burned his dwelling to the ground,
   And he was forced to fly;
So with his wife and child he fled,
Nor had he where to rest his head.

"With fire and sword the country round
   Was wasted far and wide;
And many a childing mother then
   And new-born baby died.
But things like that, you know, must be
At every famous victory.

"They say it was a shocking sight
   After the field was won;
For many thousand bodies here
   Lay rotting in the sun.
But things like that, you know, must be
After a famous victory.

"Great praise the Duke of Marlbro' won,
   And our good Prince Eugene."
"Why, 'twas a very wicked thing!"
   Said little Wilhelmine.
"Nay, nay, my little girl," quoth he,
"It was a famous victory!

"And everybody praised the Duke
   Who this great fight did win."
"But what good came of it at last?"
   Quoth little Peterkin.
"Why that I cannot tell," said he,
"But 'twas a famous victory."

ROBERT SOUTHEY

Mad Margaret's Song

Cherrily carols the lark
   Over the cot.
Merrily whistles the clark
   Scratching a blot.
     But the lark
     And the clark,
     I remark,
   Comfort me not!

Over the ripening peach
   Buzzes the bee.
Splash on the billowy beach
   Tumbles the sea.
     But the peach
     And the beach
     They are each
   Nothing to me!

W. S. GILBERT

A Tragic Story

There lived a sage in days of yore,
And he a handsome pigtail wore;
But wondered much, and sorrowed more,
  Because it hung behind him.

He mused upon this curious case,
And swore he'd change the pigtail's place,
And have it hanging at his face,
  Not dangling there behind him.

Says he, "The mystery I've found,—
I'll turn me round,"—he turned him round;
  But still it hung behind him.

Then round and round, and out and in,
All day the puzzled sage did spin;
In vain—it mattered not a pin,—
  The pigtail hung behind him.

And right, and left, and round about,
And up, and down, and in, and out
He turned; but still the pigtail stout
  Hung steadily behind him.

And though his efforts never slack,
And though he twist, and twirl, and tack,
Alas! still faithful to his back,
  The pigtail hangs behind him.

WILLIAM MAKEPEACE THACKERAY

Calico Pie

Calico Pie,
  The little Birds fly
Down to the calico tree.
  Their wings were blue
  And they sang 'Tilly-loo'—
  Till away they all flew,
And they never came back to me!
  The never came back!
  They never came back!
They never came back to me!

EDWARD LEAR

Mr. Nobody

I know a funny little man,
  As quiet as a mouse.
He does the mischief that is done
  In everybody's house.
Though no one ever sees his face,
  Yet one and all agree
That every plate we break, was cracked
  By Mr Nobody.

'Tis he who always tears our books,
  Who leaves the door ajar.
He picks the buttons from our shirts,
  And scatters pins afar.
That squeaking door will always squeak—
  For prithee, don't you see?
We leave the oiling to be done
  By Mr Nobody.

He puts damp wood upon the fire,
  That kettles will not boil:
His are the feet that bring in mud
  And all the carpets soil.
The papers that so oft are lost—
  Who had them last but he?
There's no one tosses them about
  But Mr Nobody.

The fingermarks upon the door
  By none of us were made.
We never leave the blinds unclosed
  To let the curtains fade.

The ink we never spill! The boots
  That lying round you see,
Are not our boots—they all belong
  To Mr Nobody.

Serious Omission

I know that there are dragons,
St. George's, Jason's, too,
And many modern dragons
With scales of green and blue;

But though I've been there many times
And carefully looked through,
I cannot find a dragon
In the cages at the Zoo!

JOHN FARRAR

Other Children

Little Indian, Sioux, or Crow,
Little frosty Eskimo,
Little Turk or Japanee—
Oh! don't you wish that you were me?

You have seen the scarlet trees,
And the lions overseas;
You have eaten ostrich eggs,
And turned the turtle off their legs.

Such a life is very fine,
But it's not as nice as mine;
You must often, as you trod,
Have wearied not to be abroad.

You have curious things to eat,
I am fed on proper meat;
You must dwell beyond the foam,
But I am safe and live at home.

Little Indian, Sioux, or Crow,
Little frosty Eskimo,
Little Turk or Japanee—
Oh! don't you wish that you were me?

ROBERT LOUIS STEVENSON

The Lamb

Little Lamb, who made thee?
 Dost thou know who made thee?
Gave thee life and bid thee feed
By the stream and o'er the mead;
Gave thee clothing of delight,
Softest clothing, woolly, bright;
Gave thee such a tender voice
Making all the vales rejoice?
 Little Lamb, who made thee?
 Dost thou know who made thee?

Little Lamb, I'll tell thee,
 Little Lamb, I'll tell thee:
He is callèd by thy name,
For he calls himself a Lamb.
He is meek and he is mild;
He became a litle child.
I a child and thou a lamb,
We are callèd by his name.
 Little Lamb, God bless thee.
 Little Lamb, God bless thee.

WILLIAM BLAKE

Good and Bad Children

Children, you are very little,
And your bones are very brittle;
If you would grow great and stately,
You must try to walk sedately.

You must still be bright and quiet,
And content with simple diet;
And remain, through all bewild'ring,
Innocent and honest children.

Happy hearts and happy faces,
Happy play in grassy places—
That was how, in ancient ages,
Children grew to kings and sages.

But the unkind and the unruly,
And the sort who eat unduly,
They must never hope for glory—
Theirs is quite a different story!

Cruel children, crying babies,
All grow up as geese and gabies,
Hated, as their age increases,
By their nephews and their nieces.

ROBERT LOUIS STEVENSON

Mistress Mary,
Quite contrary,
How does your garden grow?
With silver bells,
And cockle shells,
And columbines all in a row.

Mary had a little lamb,
Its fleece was white as snow;
And everywhere that Mary went,
The lamb was sure to go.

He followed her to school one day,
Which was against the rule,
It made the children laugh and play
To see a lamb at school.

The Height of the Ridiculous

I wrote some lines once on a time
   In wondrous merry mood.
And thought, as usual, men would say
   They were exceeding good.

They were so queer, so very queer,
   I laughed as I would die;
Albeit, in the general way,
   A sober man am I.

I called my servant, and he came;
   How kind it was of him
To mind a slender man like me.
   He of the mighty limb,

"These to the printer," I exclaimed.
   And, in my humorous way,
I added (as a trifling jest),
   "There'll be the devil to pay."

He took the paper, and I watched,
   And saw him peep within;
At the first line he read his face
   Was all upon the grin.

He read the next; the grin grew broad,
   And shot from ear to ear;
He read the third; a chuckling noise
   I now began to hear.

The fourth; he broke into a roar;
   The fifth; his waistband split;
The sixth; he burst five buttons off,
   And tumbled in a fit.

Ten days and nights, with sleepless eye,
   I watched that wretched man,
And since, I never dare to write
   As funny as I can.

OLIVER WENDELL HOLMES

An Elegy on the Death of a Mad Dog

Good people all, of every sort,
   Give ear unto my song;
And if you find it wondrous short,
   It cannot hold you long.

In Islington there was a man
   Of whom the world might say,
That still a godly race he ran,
   Whene'er he went to pray.

A kind and gentle heart he had,
   To comfort friends and foes:
The naked every day he clad,
   When he put on his clothes.

And in that town a dog was found,
   As many dogs there be,
Both mongrel, puppy, whelp, and hound,
   And curs of low degree.

This dog and man at first were friends;
   But when a pique began,
The dog, to gain some private ends,
   Went mad, and bit the man.

Around from all the neighboring streets
   The wondering neighbors ran,
And swore the dog had lost his wits,
   To bite so good a man.

The wound it seemed both sore and sad
   To every Christian eye:
And while they swore the dog was mad,
   They swore the man would die.

But soon a wonder came to light
   That showed the rogues they lied:
The man recovered of the bite,
   The dog it was that died.

OLIVER GOLDSMITH

Of Truth and Beauty

If there were dreams to sell,
  What would you buy?
Some cost a passing bell;
  Some a light sigh,
That shakes from Life's fresh crown
Only a roseleaf down.
If there were dreams to sell,
Merry and sad to tell,
And the crier rung the bell,
  What would you buy?

THOMAS LOVELL BEDDOES

I never saw a moor,
I never saw the sea;
Yet know I how the heather looks,
And what a wave must be.

I never spoke with God,
Nor visited in heaven;
Yet certain am I of the spot
As if the chart were given.

EMILY DICKINSON

Annabel Lee

It was many and many a year ago,
    In a kingdom by the sea,
That a maiden there lived whom you may
        know
    By the name of Annabel Lee;—
And this maiden she lived with no other
        thought
    Than to love and be loved by me.

I was a child and *she* was a child,
    In this kingdom by the sea,
But we loved with a love that was more than
        love—
    I and my Annabel Lee—
With a love that the winged seraphs in
        Heaven
    Coveted her and me.

And this was the reason that, long ago,
    In this kingdom by the sea,
A wind blew out of a cloud, chilling
    My beautiful Annabel Lee;
So that her high-born kinsmen came
    And bore her away from me,
To shut her up in a sepulcher
    In this kingdom by the sea.

EDGAR ALLAN POE

"She Walks in Beauty"

She walks in beauty, like the night
    Of cloudless climes and starry skies;
And all that's best of dark and bright
    Meet in her aspect and her eyes:
Thus mellowed to that tender light
    Which heaven to gaudy day denies.

One shade the more, one ray the less,
    Had half impaired the nameless grace
Which waves in every raven tress
    Or softly lightens o'er her face;
Where thoughts serenely sweet express
    How pure, how dear their dwelling-place.

And on that cheek, and o'er that brow
    So soft, so calm, yet eloquent,
The smiles that win, the tints that glow,
    But tell of days in goodness spent,
A mind at peace with all below,
    A heart whose love is innocent!

GEORGE GORDON BYRON

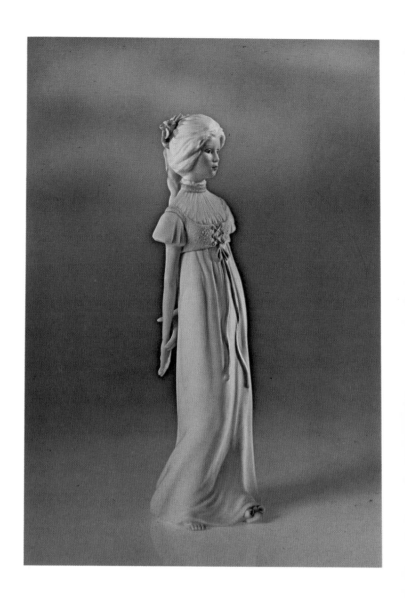

Lavender's Blue

Lavender's blue, dilly dilly: lavender's green;
When I am King, dilly dilly, you shall be Queen.
Who told you that, dilly dilly, who told you so?
'Twas my own heart, dilly dilly, that told me so.

Call up your men, dilly dilly, set them to work;
Some to the plough, dilly dilly, some to the cart;
Some to make hay, dilly dilly, some to thresh corn,
While you and I, dilly dilly, keep ourselves warm.

If I should die, dilly dilly, as well may hap,
Bury me deep, dilly dilly, under the tap;
Under the tap, dilly dilly, I'll tell you why,
That I may drink, dilly dilly, when I am dry.

The Barefoot Boy

Blessings on thee, little man,
Barefoot boy, with cheek of tan!
With thy turned-up pantaloons,
And thy merry whistled tunes;
With thy red lip, redder still
Kissed by strawberries on the hill;
With the sunshine on thy face,
Through thy torn brim's jaunty grace;
From my heart I give thee joy,—
I was once a barefoot boy!

Prince thou sat,—the grown-up man
Only is republican.
Let the million-dollared ride!
Barefoot, trudging at his side,
Thou hast more than he can buy
In the reach of ear and eye,—
Outward sunshine, inward joy:
Blessings on thee, barefoot boy!

Oh, for boyhood's painless play,
Sleep that wakes in laughing day,
Health that mocks the doctor's rules,
Knowledge never learned of schools,
Of the wild bee's morning chase,
Of the wild flower's time and place,
Flight of fowl and habitude
Of the tenants of the wood;
How the tortoise bears his shell,
How the woodchuck digs his cell,
And the ground-mole sinks his well;
How the robin feeds her young,
How the oriole's nest is hung;

Where the whitest lilies blow,
Where the freshest berries grow,
Where the ground-nut trails its vine,
Where the wood-grape's clusters shine;
Of the black wasp's cunning way,
Mason of his walls of clay,
And the architectural plans
Of gray hornet artisans!
For, eschewing books and tasks,
Nature answers all he asks;
Hand in hand with her he walks,
Face to face with her he talks,
Part and parcel of her joy,—
Blessings on the barefoot boy!

Oh, for boyhood's time of June,
Crowding years in one brief moon,
When all things I heard or saw,
Me, their master, waited for.
I was rich in flowers and trees,
Humming-birds and honey-bees;
For my sport the squirrel played,
Plied the snouted mole his spade;
For my taste the blackberry cone
Purpled over hedge and stone;
Laughed the brook for my delight
Through the day and through the night,—
Whispering at the garden wall,
Talked with me from fall to fall;
Mine the sand-rimmed pickerel pond,
Mine the walnut slopes beyond,
Mine, on bending orchard trees,
Apples of Hesperides!

JOHN GREENLEAF WHITTIER

Who has seen the wind?
   Neither I nor you;
But where the leaves hang trembling,
   The wind is passing through.
Who has seen the wind?
   Neither you nor I;
But when the trees bow down their heads,
   The wind is passing by.

CHRISTINA ROSSETTI

Summer Evening

The frog half fearful jumps across the path,
And little mouse that leaves its hole at eve
Nibbles with timid dread beneath the swath;
My rustling steps awhile their joys deceive,
Till past,—and then the cricket sings more strong,
And grasshoppers in merry moods still wear
The short night weary with their fretting song.
Up from behind the molehill jumps the hare,
Cheat of his chosen bed, and from the bank
The yellowhammer flutters in short fears
From off its nest hid in the grasses rank,
And drops again when no more noise it hears.
Thus nature's human link and endless thrall,
Proud man, still seems the enemy of all.

JOHN CLARE

84

Kubla Khan

In Xanadu did Kubla Khan
   A stately pleasure-dome decree:
Where Alph, the sacred river, ran
Through caverns measureless to man
   Down to a sunless sea.
So twice five miles of fertile ground
With walls and towers were girdled round:
And there were gardens bright with sinuous rills,
Where blossomed many an incense-bearing tree;
And here were forests ancient as the hills,
Enfolding sunny spots of greenery.

But O! that deep romantic chasm which slanted
Down the green hill athwart a cedarn cover!
A savage place! as holy and enchanted
As e'er beneath a waning moon was haunted
By woman wailing for her demon-lover!

And from this chasm, with ceaseless turmoil
   seething,
As if this Earth in fast thick pants were breathing,
A mighty fountain momently was forced,
Amid whose swift half-intermitted burst
Huge fragments vaulted like rebounding hail,
Or chaffy grain beneath the thresher's flail:
And 'mid these dancing rocks at once and ever
It flung up momently the sacred river.
Five miles meandering with a mazy motion
Through wood and dale the sacred river ran,
Then reached the caverns measureless to man,
And sank in tumult to a lifeless ocean:
And 'mid this tumult Kubla heard from far
Ancestral voices prophesying war!

   The shadow of the dome of pleasure
   Floated midway on the waves;
   Where was heard the mingled measure
   From the fountain and the caves.
It was a miracle of rare device,
A sunny pleasure-dome with caves of ice!

   A damsel with a dulcimer
   In a vision once I saw:
   It was an Abyssinian maid,
   And on her dulcimer she played,
   Singing of Mount Abora.
   Could I revive within me
   Her symphony and song,
   To such a deep delight 'twould win me

That with music loud and long,
I would build that dome in air,
That sunny dome! those caves of ice!
And all who heard should see them there,
And all should cry, Beware! Beware!
His flashing eyes, his floating hair!
Weave a circle round him thrice,
And close your eyes with holy dread,
For he on honey-dew hath fed,
And drunk the milk of Paradise.

SAMUEL TAYLOR COLERIDGE

ᘏᕞᕞᘏ

The Lady of Shalott

On either side the river lie
Long fields of barley and of rye,
That clothe the world and meet the sky;
And thro' the field the road runs by
   To many-towered Camelot;
And up and down the people go,
Gazing where the lilies blow
Round an island there below,
   The island of Shalott.

Willows whiten, aspens quiver,
Little breezes dusk and shiver
Thro' the wave that runs for ever
By the island in the river
   Flowing down to Camelot.
Four gray walls, and four gray towers,
Overlook a space of flowers,
And the silent isle imbowers
   The Lady of Shalott.

By the margin, willow-veil'd,
Slide the heavy barges trail'd
By slow horses; and unhail'd
The shallop flitteth silken-sail'd
   Skimming down to Camelot:
But who hath seen her wave her hand?
Or at the casement seen her stand?
Or is she known in all the land,
   The Lady of Shalott?

ALFRED, LORD TENNYSON

Portia's Speech

The quality of mercy is not strain'd,
It droppeth as the gentle rain from heaven
Upon the place beneath: it is twice blest;
It blesseth him that gives, and him that takes:
'Tis mightiest in the mightiest: it becomes
The throned monarch better than his crown;
His sceptre shows the force of temporal power,
The attribute to awe and majesty,
Wherein doth sit the dread and fear of kings;
But mercy is above this sceptred sway;
It is enthroned in the hearts of kings,
It is an attribute to God himself;
And earthly power doth then show likest God's
When mercy seasons justice.

WILLIAM SHAKESPEARE

Juliet

Soft! what light through yonder window breaks?
It is the east, and Juliet is the sun!
Arise, fair sun, and kill the envious moon.
Who is already sick and pale with grief,
That thou her maid are far more fair than she:
Be not her maid, since she is envious;
Her vestal livery is but sick and green,
And none but fools do wear it; cast it off.
It is my lady; O, it is my love!
O, that she knew she were!
She speaks, yet she says nothing: what of that?
Her eye discourses, I will answer it.
I am too bold, 'tis not to me she speaks:
Two of the fairest stars in all the heaven,
Having some business, do intreat her eyes
To twinkle in their spheres till they return.
What if her eyes were there, they in her head?
The brightness of her cheek would shame those
    stars
As daylight doth a lamp; her eyes in heaven
Would through the airy region stream so bright
That birds would sing and think it were not
    night.
See, how she leans her cheek upon her hand!
O, that I were a glove upon that hand,
That I might touch that cheek!

WILLIAM SHAKESPEARE

Lucy

She dwelt among the untrodden ways
    Beside the springs of Dove;
A maid whom there were none to praise,
    And very few to love.

A violet by a mossy stone
    Half hidden from the eye!
Fair as a star, when only one
    Is shining in the sky.

She lived unknown, and few could know
    When Lucy ceased to be;
But she is in her grave, and O,
    The difference to me!

WILLIAM WORDSWORTH

Jenny

Jenny kissed me when we met,
    Jumping from the chair she sat in;
Time, you thief, who love to get
    Sweets into your list, put that in:
Say I'm weary, say I'm sad,
    Say that health and wealth have missed me,
Say I'm growing old, but add
    Jenny kissed me.

LEIGH HUNT

Sylvia

Who is Sylvia, what is she,
    That all our swains commend her?
Holy, fair, and wise is she;
    The heaven such grace did lend her,
That she might admirèd be.

Is she kind as she is fair?
    For beauty lives with kindness,
Love doth to her eyes repair,
    To help him of his blindness,
And, being help'd inhabits there.

Then to Sylvia let us sing,
    That Sylvia is excelling;
She excels each mortal thing
    Upon the dull earth dwelling:
To her let us garlands bring.

WILLIAM SHAKESPEARE

Song

She is not fair to outward view
    As many maidens be,
Her loveliness I never knew
    Until she smiled on me;
Oh! then I saw her eye was bright,
A well of love, a spring of light.

But now her looks are coy and cold,
    To mine they ne'er reply,
And yet I cease not to behold
    The love-light in her eye:
Her very frowns are fairer far
Than smiles of other maidens are.

HARTLEY COLERIDGE

In a Library

A precious, mouldering pleasure 'tis
To meet an antique book,
In just the dress his century wore;
A privilege, I think,

His venerable hand to take,
And warming in our own,
A passage back, or two, to make
To times when he was young.

His quaint opinions to inspect,
His knowledge to unfold
On what concerns our mutual mind,
The literature of old;

What interested scholars most,
What competitions ran
When Plato was a certainty,
And Sophocles a man;

When Sappho was a living girl,
And Beatrice wore
The gown that Dante deified.
Facts, centuries before,

He traverses familiar,
As one should come to town
And tell you all your dreams were true:
He lived where dreams were sown.

His presence is enchantment,
You beg him not to go;
Old volumes shake their vellum heads
And tantalize, just so.

EMILY DICKINSON

If I Were a Queen

"If I were a Queen,
    What would I do?
I'd make you King,
    And I'd wait on you."

"If I were a King,
    What would I do?
I'd make you Queen,
    For I'd marry you."

CHRISTINA ROSSETTI

A Lady Sweet and Kind

There is a lady sweet and kind,
Was never face so pleased my mind;
I did but see her passing by,
And yet I love her till I die.

Her gesture, motion, and her smiles,
Her wit, her voice my heart beguiles,
Beguiles my heart, I know not why,
And yet I love her till I die.

On a Certain Lady at Court

I know a thing that's most uncommon;
   (Envy, be silent and attend!)
I know a reasonable woman,
   Handsome and witty, yet a friend.

Not warped by passion, awed by rumor;
   Not grave through pride, nor gay through folly;
An equal mixture of good-humor
   And sensible soft melancholy.

"Has she no faults then (Envy says), Sir?"
   Yes, she has one, I must aver:
When all the world conspires to praise her,
   The woman's deaf, and does not hear.

ALEXANDER POPE

The Piper's Song

Piping down the valleys wild,
   Piping songs of pleasant glee,
On a cloud I saw a child,
   And he laughing said to me:

"Pipe a song about a lamb!"
   So I piped with merry cheer.
"Piper, pipe that song again;"
   So I piped: he wept to hear.

"Drop thy pipe, thy happy pipe;
   Sing thy songs of happy cheer!"
So I sang the same again,
   While he wept with joy to hear.

"Piper, sit thee down and write
   In a book that all may read."
So he vanished from my sight;
   And I plucked a hollow reed,

And I made a rural pen,
   And I stained the water clear,
And I wrote my happy songs
   Every child may joy to hear.

WILLIAM BLAKE

91

A Cradle Song

Sweet dreams, form a shade
O'er my lovely infant's head;
Sweet dreams of pleasant streams
By happy, silent, moony beams.

Sweet sleep, with soft down
Weave thy brows an infant crown,
Sweet sleep, Angel mild,
Hover o'er my happy child.

Sweet smiles, in the night
Hover over my delight;
Sweet smiles, mother's smiles,
All the livelong night beguiles.

Sweet moans, dovelike sighs,
Chase not slumber from thy eyes.
Sweet moans, sweeter smiles,
All the dovelike moans beguiles.

Sleep, sleep, happy child,
All creation slept and smiled;
Sleep, sleep, happy sleep,
While o'er thee thy mother weep.

Sweet babe, in thy face
Holy image I can trace.
Sweet babe, once like thee,
Thy Maker lay and wept for me,

Wept for me, for thee, for all,
When He was an infant small.
Thou His image ever see,
Heavenly face that smiles on thee,

Smiles on thee, on me, on all;
Who became an infant small.
Infant smiles are His own smiles;
Heaven and earth to peace beguiles.

WILLIAM BLAKE

Words to Live By

Hope is the thing with feathers
That perches in the soul,
And sings the tune without the words,
And never stops at all,

And sweetest in the gale is heard;
And sore must be the storm
That could abash the little bird
That kept so many warm.

I've heard it in the chillest land,
And on the strangest sea;
Yet, never, in extremity,
It asked a crumb of me.

EMILY DICKINSON

Sweet Are the Thoughts

Sweet are the thoughts that savour of content;
  The quiet mind is richer than a crown.
Sweet are the nights in careless slumber spent;
  The poor estate scorns fortune's angry frown.
Such sweet content, such minds, such sleep, such
      bliss
  Beggars enjoy when princes oft do miss.

The homely house that harbours quiet rest,
  The cottage that affords no pride nor care,
The mean that 'grees with country music best,
  The sweet consort of mirth and music's fare,
Obscured life sets down a type of bliss;
  A mind content, both crown and kingdom is.

ROBERT GREENE

The Happiest Heart

Who drives the horses of the sun
  Shall lord it but a day;
Better the lowly deed were done,
  And kept the humble way.

The rust will find the sword of fame,
  The dust will hide the crown;
Aye, none shall nail so high his name
  Time will not tear it down.

The happiest heart that ever beat
  Was in some quiet breast
That found the common daylight sweet,
  And left to Heaven the rest.

JOHN VANCE CHENEY

94

Auguries of Innocence

To see a World in a Grain of Sand,
And a Heaven in a Wild Flower,
Hold Infinity in the palm of your hand,
And Eternity in an hour.

A Robin Redbreast in a Cage
Puts all Heaven in a Rage.
A dove-house fill'd with Doves and Pigeons
Shudders Hell thro' all its regions.

A dog starv'd at his Master's Gate
Predicts the ruin of the State.
A Horse misused upon the Road
Calls to Heaven for Human blood.

Each outcry of the hunted Hare
A fibre from the Brain does tear.
A Skylark wounded in the wing;
A Cherubim does cease to sing.

He who shall hurt the little Wren
Shall never be belov'd by Men.
He who the Ox to wrath has mov'd
Shall never be by Woman lov'd.

The wanton Boy that kills the Fly
Shall feel the Spider's enmity. . . .
The Beggar's Dog and Widow's Cat,
Feed them and thou wilt grow fat.

A Truth that's told with bad intent
Beats all the Lies you can invent.
It is right it should be so;
Man was made for Joy and Woe;
And when this we rightly know,
Thro' the World we safely go.

Every Night and every Morn
Some to Misery are born.
Every Morn and every Night
Some are Born to Sweet Delight.
Some are Born to Sweet Delight,
Some are Born to Endless Night.

WILLIAM BLAKE

95

To Make a Prairie

To make a prairie it takes a clover and one bee,—
One clover, and a bee,
And revery.
The revery alone will do
If bees are few.

EMILY DICKINSON

Lost

I lost a world the other day.
Has anybody found?
You'll know it by the row of stars
Around its forehead bound.

A rich man might not notice it;
Yet to my frugal eye
Of more esteem than ducats.
Oh, find it, sir, for me!

EMILY DICKINSON

The Night Has a Thousand Eyes

The night has a thousand eyes,
    And the day but one;
Yet the light of the bright world dies
    With the dying sun.

The mind has a thousand eyes,
    And the heart but one;
Yet the light of a whole life dies
    When love is done.

FRANCIS WILLIAM BOURDILLON

A Lesson

A Toadstool comes up in a night,—
    Learn the lesson, little folk:
An oak grows on a hundred years,
    But then it is an oak.

CHRISTINA ROSSETTI

Four Things

Four things a man must learn to do
If he would make his record true:
To think without confusion clearly;
To love his fellow-men sincerely;
To act from honest motives purely;
To trust in God and Heaven securely.

HENRY VAN DYKE

Evolution

Out of the dusk a shadow,
    Then, a spark;
Out of the cloud a silence,
    Then, a lark;
Out of the heart a rapture,
    Then, a pain;
Out of the dead, cold ashes,
    Life again.

JOHN BANISTER TABB

I Saw a Man

I saw a man pursuing the horizon;
Round and round they sped.
I was disturbed at this;
I accosted the man.
"It is futile," I said,
"You can never—"

"You lie," he cried,
And ran on.

STEPHEN CRANE

Sound the Clarion

Sound, sound the clarion, fill the fife!
    To all the sensual world proclaim,
One crowded hour of glorious life
    Is worth an age without a name.

SIR WALTER SCOTT

96

Abou Ben Adhem

Abou Ben Adhem (may his tribe increase!)
Awoke one night from a deep dream of peace,
And saw within the moonlight in his room,
Making it rich and like a lily in bloom,
An angel writing in a book of gold:
Exceeding peace had made Ben Adhem bold,
And to the presence in the room he said,
"What writest thou?" The vision raised its head,
And, with a look made of all sweet accord,
Answered, "The names of those who love the
    Lord."
"And is mine one?" said Abou. "Nay, not so,"
Replied the angel. Abou spoke more low,
But cheerily still; and said, "I pray thee, then,
Write me as one that loves his fellow-men."

The angel wrote, and vanished. The next night
It came again, with a great wakening light,
And showed the names whom love of God had
    blessed,—
And, lo! Ben Adhem's name led all the rest!

LEIGH HUNT

Courage!

Say not, the struggle naught availeth,
    The labor and the wounds are vain,
The enemy faints not, nor faileth,
    And as things have been they remain.

If hopes were dupes, fears may be liars;
    It may be, in yon smoke concealed,
Your comrades chase e'en now the fliers,
    And, but for you, possess the field.

For while the tired waves, vainly breaking,
    Seem here no painful inch to gain,
Far back, through creeks and inlets making,
    Comes silent, flooding in, the main.

And not by eastern windows only,
    When daylight comes, comes in the light;
In front, the sun climbs slow, how slowly!
    But westward, look, the land is bright!

ARTHUR HUGH CLOUGH

So Nigh Is Grandeur

In an age of fops and toys,
Wanting wisdom, void of right,
Who shall nerve heroic boys
To hazard all in Freedom's fight,—
Break sharply off their jolly games,
Forsake their comrades gay
And quit proud homes and youthful dames
For famine, toil and fray?
Yet on the nimble air benign
Speed nimbler messages,
That waft the breath of grace divine
To hearts in sloth and ease.
So nigh is grandeur to our dust,
So near is God to man,
When Duty whispers low, *Thou must,*
The youth replies, *I can.*

RALPH WALDO EMERSON

Invictus

Out of the night that covers me,
    Black as the pit from pole to pole,
I thank whatever gods may be,
    For my unconquerable soul.

In the fell clutch of circumstance
    I have not winced nor cried aloud.
Under the bludgeonings of chance
    My head is bloody but unbowed.

Beyond this place of wrath and tears
    Looms but the horror of the shade,
And yet the menace of the years
    Finds and shall find me unafraid.

It matters not how straight the gate
    How charged with punishments the scroll,
I am the master of my fate,
    I am the captain of my soul.

WILLIAM ERNEST HENLEY

The Old Philosopher

I strove with none, for none was worth my strife:
    Nature I loved, and next to Nature, Art:
I warmed both hands before the fire of Life;
    It sinks; and I am ready to depart.

WALTER SAVAGE LANDOR

97

Pearl Seed

Songs are sung in my mind
　　As pearls are formed in the sea;
Each thought with thy name entwined
　　Becomes a sweet song in me.

Dimly those pale pearls shine,
　　Hidden under the sea,—
Vague are those songs of mine,
　　So deeply they lie in me.

CHARLES KINGSLEY

Stupidity Street

I saw with open eyes
Singing birds sweet
Sold in the shops
For the people to eat,
Sold in the shops of
Stupidity Street.

I saw in a vision
The worm in the wheat,
And in the shops nothing
For people to eat:
Nothing for sale in
Stupidity Street.

RALPH HODGSON

The Example

Here's an example from
　　A Butterfly;
That on a rough, hard rock
　　Happy can lie;
Friendless and all alone
On this unsweetened stone.

Now let my bed be hard
　　No care take I;
I'll make my joy like this
　　Small Butterfly;
Whose happy heart has power
To make a stone a flower.

WILLIAM H. DAVIES

Ode on Solitude

Happy the man whose wish and care
　　A few paternal acres bound,
Content to breathe his native air
　　In his own ground:

Whose herds with milk, whose fields with bread,
　　Whose flocks supply him with attire;
Whose trees in summer yield him shade,
　　In winter fire:

Blest, who can unconcern'dly find
　　Hours, days, and years slide soft away;
In health of body, peace of mind,
　　Quiet by day:

Sound sleep by night, study and ease,
　　Together mixt, sweet recreation;
And innocence, which most does please,
　　With meditation.

Thus let me live, unseen, unknown;
　　Thus, unlamented, let me die,
Steal from the world, and not a stone
　　Tell where I lie.

ALEXANDER POPE

Young and Old

When all the world is young, lad,
　　And all the trees are green;
And every goose a swan, lad,
　　And every lass a queen;
Then hey for boot and horse, lad,
　　And round the world away;
Young blood must have its course, lad,
　　And every dog his day.

When all the world is old, lad,
　　And all the trees are brown;
And all the sport is stale, lad,
　　And all the wheels run down:
Creep home, and take your place there,
　　The spent and maimed among:
God grant you find one face there
　　You loved when all was young.

CHARLES KINGSLEY

Little Things

Little things, that run, and quail,
And die, in silence and despair!

Little things, that fight, and fail,
And fall, on sea, and earth, and air!

All trapped and frightened little things,
The mouse, the coney, hear our prayer!

As we forgive those done to us,
—The lamb, the linnet, and the hare—

Forgive us all our trespasses,
Little creatures, everywhere!

JAMES STEPHENS

Lend a Hand

Look up! and not down;
Out! and not in;
Forward! and not back;
And lend a hand.

EDWARD EVERETT HALE

Rainbow in the Sky

My heart leaps up when I behold
    A rainbow in the sky:
So was it when my life began;
So is it now I am a man;
So be it when I shall grow old,
    Or let me die!

WILLIAM WORDSWORTH

Happy Thought

The world is so full of a number of things,
I'm sure we should all be as happy as kings.

ROBERT LOUIS STEVENSON

Compassion

Hurt no living thing:
    Ladybird, nor butterfly,
Nor moth with dusty wing,
    No cricket chirping cheerily,
Nor grasshopper so light of leap,
    Nor dancing gnat, no beetle fat,
Nor harmless worms that creep.

CHRISTINA ROSSETTI

99

Eldorado

Gayly bedight,
  A gallant knight,
In sunshine and in shadow,
  Had journeyed long,
  Singing a song,
In search of Eldorado.

But he grew old—
  This knight so bold—
And o'er his heart a shadow
  Fell as he found
  No spot of ground
That looked like Eldorado.

And, as his strength
  Failed him at length,
He met a pilgrim shadow.
  "Shadow," said he,
  "Where can it be—
This land of Eldorado?"

"Over the Mountains
  Of the Moon,
Down the Valley of the Shadow,
  Ride, boldly ride,"
  The shade replied,
"If you seek for Eldorado!"

EDGAR ALLAN POE

Requiem

Under the wide and starry sky,
Dig the grave and let me lie.
Glad did I live and gladly die,
  And I laid me down with a will.

This be the verse you grave for me:
Here he lies where he longed to be,
Home is the sailor, home from sea,
  And the hunter home from the hill.

ROBERT LOUIS STEVENSON

Opportunity

This I beheld, or dreamed it in a dream:—
There spread a cloud of dust along a plain;
And underneath the cloud, or in it, raged

A furious battle, and men yelled, and swords
Shocked upon swords and shields. A prince's banner
Wavered, then staggered backward, hemmed by foes.
A craven hung along the battle's edge,
And thought, "Had I a sword of keener steel—
That blue blade that the king's son bears,—but this
Blunt thing!" he snapped and flung it from his hand,
And lowering crept away and left the field.
Then came the king's son, wounded, sore bestead,
And weaponless, and saw the broken sword,
Hilt-buried in the dry and trodden sand,
And ran and snatched it, and with battle-shout
Lifted afresh he hewed his enemy down,
And saved a great cause that heroic day.

EDWARD ROWLAND SILL

Courage

Courage is armor
A blind man wears;
The calloused scar
Of outlived despairs:
Courage is Fear
That has said its prayers.

KARLE WILSON BAKER

The Arrow and the Song

I shot an arrow into the air,
It fell to earth, I knew not where;
For, so swiftly it flew, the sight
Could not follow it in its flight.

I breathed a song into the air,
It fell to earth, I knew not where;
For who has sight so keen and strong,
That it can follow the flight of song?

Long, long afterward, in an oak
I found the arrow, still unbroke;
And the song, from beginning to end,
I found again in the heart of a friend.

HENRY WADSWORTH LONGFELLOW

Hail Columbia

Hail, Columbia! happy land!
Hail, ye heroes! heaven-born band!
  Who fought and bled in freedom's cause,
  Who fought and bled in freedom's cause,
And when the storm of war was gone,
Enjoyed the peace your valor won.
  Let independence be our boast,
  Ever mindful what it cost;
  Every grateful for the prize,
  Let its altar reach the skies.

Cho.: Firm, united, let us be,
      Rallying round our liberty;
      As a band of brothers joined,
      Peace and safety we shall find.

Immortal patriots! rise once more:
Defend your rights, defend your shore:
  Let no rude foe, with impious hand,
  Let no rude foe, with impious hand,
Invade the shrine where sacred lies
Of toil and blood the well-earned prize.
  While offering peace sincere and just,
  In Heaven we place a manly trust,
  That truth and justice will prevail,
  And every scheme of bondage fail.

JOSEPH HOPKINSON

I Hear America Singing

I hear America singing, the varied carols I hear,
Those of mechanics, each one singing his as it
  should be, blithe and strong.
The carpenter singing his as he measures his
  plank or beam,
The mason singing as he makes ready for work,
  or leaves off work.
The boatman singing what belongs to him in the
  boat, the deckhand singing on the steamboat
  deck,
The shoemaker singing as he sits on his bench,
  the hatter singing as he stands,
The woodcutter's song, the ploughboy's on his
  way in the morning, or at noon intermission, or at
  sundown,
The delicious singing of the mother, or of the
  young wife at work, or of the girl singing or
  washing,
Each singing what belongs to him or her and to
  none else,
The day that belongs to the day—at night the
  party of young fellows, robust, friendly,
Singing with open mouths their strong, melodious
  songs.

WALT WHITMAN

Day's End

Night is come,
   Owls are out;
Beetles hum
   Round about.

Children snore
   Safe in bed;
Nothing more
   Need be said.

HENRY NEWBOLT

Index of Titles

Index of First Lines

Index of Authors